W

Words that I live by
Joseph Wooten Wisdom

Dedications:
This book is dedicated to my mother, Dorothy Graye Wooten and my father Elijah Payneman Wooten aka "Pete".

Acknowledgements:
First, I thank God.

I thank my parents.
Dorothy Graye Wooten, thank you for letting your sons know that no one on Earth was better than us and simultaneously bestowing upon us humility. You are the wisest woman I have ever known.
Elijah Payneman Wooten aka "Pete", thank you for allowing all of your sons to pursue music without judgment or obstruction. Thank you for protecting us, and thank you for giving me your sense of humor.

I thank my brothers.
Elijah Reginald Wooten aka "Regi", my oldest brother and my first music teacher, thank you for picking my instrument, for teaching me keyboard playing, and expertly teaching me music theory. Thank you for giving my life direction and a career.
Roy Wilfred Wooten aka "Futureman", thank you for showing me the power of thought, deep thought. Thank you for always being behind me. Your endorsement does and always has meant so much to me.
Rudy Lovell Wooten, thank you for always caring for me. When I had the worst asthma, NO ONE ever wished they could take my place so that I could be well. You were the most loving person that I have ever known.
Victor Lemonte Wooten, you are the only little brother that I have and yet you are still like my big brother. When we were kids on the playground picking teams, I used to say, "Let me have Victor, and

you can pick whoever you like." I still feel the same way. I never lose with Victor on my team.

I thank my sons.
Jessie Joseph Wooten, you are my eldest and have always been self-motivated and self-disciplined.
Justice William-Aaron Wooten, you have always been a champion on and off the track.
Both of you make me prouder than you know.

I thank my wife.
Stephanie Ann Wooten.
You are the smartest woman and a world-class multitasker. You have the biggest heart and a smile that brightens any room. Your energy is abundant and infectious. Marrying you was the best thing I could have ever done.
You make me better.
I will love you forever.

I thank Steve Miller.
Thank you for enabling me to be part of your legendary Steve Miller Band! I joined the group in 1993, and it remains quite the honor still…after all of these years.

Thank you to all who have believed in me.
I cannot name you all, but KNOW that your endorsement is very much appreciated and humbles me.

Foreword:
By Victor Wooten

Joseph Allen Wooten has always been an extraordinary person. When his parents were pregnant with him, his three older brothers asked mom and dad to bring home a "super hero" from the hospital. The brothers - Elijah (Regi), Roy, and Rudy - say that is exactly who they got when baby Joseph arrived on December 15th, 1961.

The fourth born of five brothers, Joseph's childhood continued with frequent hospital visits due to his severe asthma. Often faced with shortness of breath, Joseph learned to make every breath and every moment count. As an infant, he surprised his parents by imitating the sounds of other babies. By age seven, he was already the keyboardist and lead vocalist in The Wooten Brothers band, which earned him the nickname, "The Voice of Gold" and as he is stilled called today, "The Hands of Soul." In his early twenties, he composed, orchestrated, and performed a show consisting of over forty original songs written for each cast member, wardrobe staff, and office personnel at Busch Gardens The Old Country in Williamsburg, Virginia. Currently, as an adult, Joseph is a father, husband, musician, songwriter, comedian, motivational speaker, sports fan, author, and more. Most importantly, (at least, to me,) Joseph Allen Wooten is my older brother.

For me, growing up with four older brothers was a blessing. The five of us were always kind and caring towards each other. I was at least twelve before I realized most brothers aren't as nice to each other as we were – especially to their younger siblings. My four older brothers were (and still are) like four extra parents to me. They've shaped the way I think, act, play, and teach in life and in music. I get a lot of credit for what I do, but I would be doing none of it if it weren't for my brothers.

Although the five of us are separated by only eight years, Joseph was the only brother I ever attended school with. Because he and I are only three years apart, we attended elementary and high school together. During those years, Joseph was a constant role model. He was also the inspiration for many of my childhood choices, such as playing soccer, running track, competing in the high jump, and joining the school choir. He continues to have that same effect on me today.

As kids, we did things other kids didn't. This allowed us to form views about ourselves and the world at an earlier age than most. These early experiences also helped form a bond between us brothers that most don't have, and that bond is everlasting.

You must realize that us five brothers were playing music together at a very early age. With our parent's guidance, we toured the west coast in the early 70s as the opening band for the legendary soul artist Curtis Mayfield. I was six years old and Joseph was nine, but he was already fronting the band singing James Brown songs – screams, attitude, and all.

The combination of touring, along with performing in nightclubs, bars, and theaters, provided opportunities for us to see a lot. Aside from going to public school, our additional life provided an additional education. Having exceptional parents was the key. Being carefully and strategically guided by them allowed us to flow safely through these experiences. As well as our physical safety, our parents were also concerned with how we processed things in our minds. They didn't hide much from us. At least, I don't think they did. So, we often talked about our experiences. They asked us many questions. To them, that was very important. Surprisingly, with all the things we saw and experienced as kids, none of us grew up to smoke, drink, or curse. That, to me, is phenomenal! Well done Mom and Dad.

It was these early life experiences combined with the guidance of our parents and older siblings that formed Joseph's way of thinking. Anyone who follows him on Facebook (www.facebook.com/Hands.of.Soul) or any other social media knows that whatever he writes is worth reading and sharing. I often share his posts instead of writing my own. Joseph always says it better. Even when people disagree with him, he handles every situation and treats each person with care, grace, and respect.

> *"A word is a vessel for meaning like a cup is a vessel for a drink. Words alone cannot give you anymore than a cup alone will quench your thirst."*

These are Joseph's words, and as you can see, they cause one to ponder. This book, **"It All Matters"** is a powerful collection of his original thoughts. It's insightful, educational, and an enjoyable read for the whole family, but be ready to think. After you read it, please re-read it and share it with your friends. Better yet, share it with your enemies. Share it with the world. As our mom would say, *"Why spend so much time doing anything if it doesn't make the world better?"* Joseph has spent his life fulfilling mom's words. This book is just one of his many ways of doing that.

Once you are finished reading, purchase Joseph's music and listen to the lyrics. Although this is his first book, he's been writing good stuff since he was a child. You can also hear him play and sing live with the Steve Miller Band (he's been Steve's keyboardist since 1993.) Definitely follow Joseph on social media. Then, you will have a glimpse into my childhood. If you follow my career and like what I do, you will *love* Joseph! And keep in mind; I have three more brothers who are just as inspiring!

Enjoy,

Victor L Wooten

(Joseph's little brother)

The ideas in this publication are not separated by category nor order of importance. They are presented to you in the same order that I documented them in my own personal handwritten book. I hope that you enjoy them. I hope that they make you think. I hope that through these thoughts and concepts you get to know me a little better. I believe that people who don't communicate to each other nor attempt to get to know one another are more likely to be divided. Here's to the beginning of healing that division.

Please enjoy...

It All Matters

IT ALL MATTERS

You weren't perfect but
    You weren't supposed to be
That's why you mean
    The most to me
Somebody tried to say
    You wasn't close to me
But they were wrong Daddy
    They were wrong Daddy

—

In the small picture the boat rocks. In the big picture the river is still steady.

—

No one should say anything about what is wrong with kids without talking about what is wrong with adults in the same sentence. Kids are the fruit. Adults are the tree. You can't talk about bad fruit without first looking at the tree.

—

Why must the nightingale tell the cricket or the frog that they are not good singers? There is enough room for everybody.

—

I once heard somebody ask Victor how he felt about a bad review someone wrote about him. Victor said, "The same way I feel about the good ones."

—

Every sunrise and sunset will be glorious to you the moment you realize that you don't have many left. Why wait until then?

—

The ones who mean the most to you don't have to tell you all the time.

—

Optimism is its own reward.
Pessimism is its own reward.

—

Of all the gifts of character that I seek, I seek clarity the most.

—

Real Beauty is not only skin deep.

—

Everything is nothing, and Nothing is everything.

—

How you will be remembered is not entirely up to you.

—

We believe in the power of evil.
We hope for the power of good.

—

The musical style a musician hates is almost always a style he/she doesn't do well.

———

A good singer shows you how great he or she is by what they do with their voice.
A great singer shows you how great the song is with their voice…and THAT shows you the greatness of their artistry.

———

True friendship is love without the compulsion.
Friendship accepts where love demands.

———

If the Bible is "the greatest story ever told" and we are a continuation of that story, then that implies that we in the story are characters.

What is a character? A character is someone who plays a role for the purpose of the story but has a reality truer than the role they play. A character has an identity that exists outside of the story. We pour our hearts and souls into our roles, even lose ourselves in them, and only within the story can we be held responsible for our actions. All of the great actors lose themselves in their roles.

A story is also written before the creation of the characters, and so is the outcome. It is not up to the character to decide his or her lines or his or her role. An actor who understands his or her role will inevitably perform better within the story and enrich the true identity.

The actor who argues with the director is out of line and only does harm to himself. The director and writer of the story remain unphased.

Life's greatest villain is "Satan", the Devil. His anguish brings life's greatest lessons. Addiction, sadness, evil, jealousy, etc…

We learn most when we hit rock bottom. Satan is the main character and is always highly impacting the outcome. It is no wonder that the Devil is played by God's greatest angel.

Eternal damnation for behavior within the story? Should Anthony Hopkins burn forever for the crimes of Hannibal Lechter?

The "story" exists for something. Its purpose, I don't know. Our roles should be taken seriously. This life within the tale is finite. Finiteness contains the Truth, because Truth is infinite, without limit. This life is a teacher of many things with a purpose set by something or someone powerfully wondrous. Live It well!

—

Love does not always demand. Friendship never does.

—

A man let out of prison cherishes his freedom. Why shouldn't I to the same degree?

—

The center of the circle contains both zero longitude and zero latitude…both 100% longitude and 100% latitude. Only in the center is nothing truly everything or everything is truly nothing.

—

Why do we fill our bodies with garbage food with no worries and then worry about opening the bathroom door with a paper towel?

—

I once heard a man speaking about "God's Law". I thought to myself, "He probably doesn't even understand the law of what to do at a four way stop."

Being onstage is a performance
A beautiful lie
A fabrication for the right reason

—

   Many people have seen me with asthma and hoped that I got
better. Only my brother, Rudy would look at me and say, "Ugh! I
wish it was me…"
Now THAT is love! (No wonder Lovell was his middle name.)

—

You can love someone at first sight, but relationships take time.

—

   Talent is to career what an acorn is to a tree. Talent can eventually
become a career, but like a tree it requires nurturing, the proper
conditions, and above all, it takes time.

—

(HIM)   "When I first met her I knew she was the one, so I married
her right away."
(ME)   "When you first picked up a bass, you knew it was the
instrument for you too, didn't you?"
(HIM)   "Yes"
(Me)   "But it was too early to start booking gigs at that time,
wasn't it?"

—

Who is smarter? The scientist who can tell you everything about the
tree or the hobo who lays under it for shade on a hot day?

—

We search for the truth when we ARE the truth. The search for truth is like a diamond in search of a dollar.

—

The only difference between the rational thinker and the fanatic is that the rational thinker holds open the possibility that he can be wrong. You can say the grass is green and be right. Upon further investigation you see that it appears green, because it soaks up every color of the spectrum except green…and if you leave the atmosphere all color goes away.

Truth should always be open-ended and leave room for it to grow. It may look green. It is actually everything except green!

—

No man is a star while scooping the cat box.

—

If you live to be 100 you will live 36,525 days.
If you had a dollar for every day of your life to 100 and you knew you would not get anymore, I guarantee you that you would be more mindful of what you do with your money than what you do right now with your time.

—

It is not enough to just know the truth. You also have to have the truth in perspective. You can say, "This is my finger," and you would be right. But if you hold the finger too close to your eyes, you start bumping into people and falling down stairs…all based on your perspective to the truth.

No law is absolute…including this one.

—

Evil triumphs because we respect it more than goodness. A man murders a famous person, and we call him by all three names. Lee Harvey Oswald, John Wilkes Booth, John Wayne Gacy, etc…

A teacher changes a life, or a millionaire shares his wealth with the needy, or a doctor gives away his expertise at no cost in relative anonymity. We don't like evil but we give it our respect.

—

Never let a horn player count off "Cherokee".
(I did not write this one, but I love it!)

—

When a woman says, "We need to talk", what she is really saying is, "We need to talk about you!"

—

The young boy who is told not to be a "cry baby" too often turns into the adult not in touch with his emotions.

—

When you improvise, it is a combination of you playing the music and the music playing you. Life is the same way. It is an improvisation, a combination of making decisions and being guided.

—

People who don't have a problem with themselves generally don't have a problem with other people.

—

Having balance is a simple premise, but the higher you rise, the more essential it becomes.

—

Do not confuse words with meaning. Words contain meaning like a cup contains a drink. You cannot quench your thirst with a cup alone. Words alone mean nothing.

Some say the Bible is the "Word of God"...as if that implies that the mere word makes it absolutely right. But words have the meaning that WE give them. WE are their meaning. The word without us is as useless as a goblet with no drink when you are thirsty.

—

A word is a vessel for meaning like a cup is a vessel for a drink. Words alone cannot give you anymore than a cup alone will quench your thirst.

—

When emotions run high, the thought process blurs, similar to how intense heat blurs vision.

—

We often see in others the problems that we ourselves have.

—

Kids are the fruit. Adults are the tree. The quality of the fruit reflects the quality of the tree.

—

Parenting, not the Peace Corp, is the toughest job you will ever love.

—

Birth is not the beginning, and death is not the end.

—

In life, some things get better and some things get worse. And some things get worse BECAUSE some things are getting better.

—

Love can be as intoxicating as any liquor.

—

Clarity is the character that focuses all other characters.

—

If we need meat for protein, why do all animals that that eat meat eat animals that don't eat meat for protein?

—

Let your friends help you when they request. If to give is to receive, then it must follow that sometimes to receive is to give.

—

There is no numeral more powerful than the zero. Without it, ALL number lines and all numbers cease to exist.

—

We, too often, under value the things that we have a lot of.

—

Sometimes love is more of a four letter word than others.

—

Wisdom is not merely following your heart. Nor is it just the navigating of the details of life with the sharp precision of the intellect. True wisdom is knowing the proper proportion of heart and head to apply to any given moment.

—

Life is what you make it.
It's real unless you fake it.

—

Zero is more than nothing. It is the basis for everything. It is the reason for everything.

—

Not everything that is understood should be put into words.

—

Words are not the same as meaning.
Talent is not the same as career.
Relationship is not the same as love.

—

A man speaks to his wife and wants her to hear what he is saying. A woman speaks to hear husband and wants him to know how she feels.

—

The center is the only place without opposite. Love resides in the center.

—

What is eternal can have no opposite. Love is eternal. Some would say hate is the opposite of love. I say hate is temporary, limited. It will have no meaning eventually.

Hate is to love what shadow is to light. Shadows, at best, can only hide from light. They can only hide behind objects, exist only where light allows. Light dissipates darkness, not with a battle, but only by being itself.

—

Love and hate are opposites only in terms of how eternal is opposite to temporary. Can temporary and eternal co-exist? Yes, temporarily…

—

There is no rebuttal to the experience of good music.

—

The best teacher is one who escorts the student on his or her journey inward.

—

Real teaching is not merely the teacher connecting the student to the teacher's concepts. Real teaching is the teacher using concepts to connect the student with himself or herself.

—

The goal of a teacher is to get the student to a point that he or she does not need that teacher anymore.

—

Concepts are finite tools. And like any tool, it is meant to be put down after its job is done.

—

Concepts are useful tools but meant to be put down eventually, like a canoe that saves your life carrying you to the shore. You love the canoe for saving you, but if you don't let go of it after you get out of the water, it becomes a burden and a hinderance.

—

Your life is a few thousand days. You will not get any more than that. Be as wise and careful with your days as you would be with a few thousand dollars if you knew you wouldn't get more.

—

Eat food that looks like food.

—

Nutrition is a study with which we should all be familiar.

—

The search for truth is a journey to yourself, your true inner core, because in the center everything connects.

—

Everyone is crazy from someone's point of view.

—

All of life is love and the lessons thereof.

—

Stevie Wonder is great not only because of the number of great songs he has written. He is also great because of the number of ways in which his music excels. Very seldom do his styles overlap. (It is not just coincidence that he is a great person.)

—

I see no problem with hyphenated Americans. Jewish-American, African-American, Italian-American, etc. Some say, "why can't we all just be American?" I say, for the same reason that a brain cell can't show up in the lung and be what it should be to the human body. My bone cells cannot show up in my skin saying, "Why can't we all just be Joseph Wooten?" Cells share the same DNA, but they are of many different types for the benefit of the whole body.

—

A quiet focused mind is the starting point and the destination.

—

At the moment you experience pain, you have already endured it. The unbearable part of pain largely is in the idea that it may not cease. Pain in the now has been endured the moment it is felt. Your idea of how long you think the pain will last makes it bearable or unbearable.

To deal with pain, do not try to fight it. Accept it. Try to focus in on it with detail, the pain that you feel right NOW, not on how long it has been hurting or on how much longer it feels like it will go on. "Now" pain you have already survived.

Accept your pain. Whatever the severity of it, and know that what you feel right now has been endured the moment you feel it.

———

Not all of the faces of love look like love.

———

If your body is a temple, then your nutrition should be as important as your religion.

———

I am destined to do great things.

———

Let my life and my music inspire.

———

The best thing that you can offer you children is a good example.

———

Your kids learn much more from watching what you do than listening to what you have to tell them.

———

People who are truly in love don't have to say it all the time…but it certainly doesn't hurt.

—

It is only considered work if you would rather be doing something else.

—

Knowing when not to speak is as important, sometimes more important than having something to say.

—

The rests are equally as important as the notes. It is the rests and the spaces between notes that differentiate great playing from merely the right notes.

—

Victory brings reward. Failure brings lessons.

—

Pay attention to the different people who enter your life. All have entered for a purpose.

—

Illness is your body's attempt to get well.

—

Life is short, but it is long enough to still want to get it right.

—

When you are not sure what to do next, don't do anything and your next move will become apparent.

—

The words, "I love you" are only effective if the one you say it to believes it already.

—

Very early in the morning is nothing but very late at night in disguise.

—

A man who believes something and does not hold open the possibility of being wrong at all is a fanatic.

—

The center of the circle does not DO anything, but its existence allows or makes possible all of the activity within the circle.

—

Earth, Wind, & Fire without Maurice White is like the show, "Good Times" without John Amos.

—

You only get a certain amount of sunrises and sunsets.

—

A word is not the same thing as meaning any more than a chalice is the same as thirst quenching water. Words are vessels and WE provide their meaning.

—

Women have meters. Men have on/off switches and yes/no buttons.

—

Human beings in essence are merely living points of view, and the "truth" that we try to communicate is merely our opinion based on our unique perspective.

—

To be right, someone else does NOT have to be wrong. The same motion of clockwise is counter-clockwise on the other side of the clock face. It's truth depends only own your perspective…and perspective is a choice.

—

As far as politics goes, I don't like to pick a side before I know the issue.

—

Asthma has been my greatest teacher.

—

If classical music is the beauty of a baby, then funk music is the blood and mucus covering that baby at birth. Funk is the placenta and the mucus plug that precedes the birth. Heck, funk is the lovemaking that made that baby possible.

—

Pepe Le Pew is totally in love and totally inconsiderate. Make sure your love considers the feelings of your person of affection.

—

I can't be Pepe Le Pew
   I've gotta think about you
And whether or not you love me too.

—

I think the Zero loves us, because it holds our universe together, our atoms together, our world together. It provides us literally everything by its connection to all.

—

Love is connection. It can be expressed as emotion, but it is more than that. True love does not love "because". It just loves. It is connected and love flows through that connection...

—

The Zero needs the one for it to express itself as oxygen, but it does not need the one for it to be Zero. The one needs the Zero for one to express itself as oxygen, and it also needs the Zero to be its singular self. One cannot be one without Zero. Zero can be Zero without one.

—

Zero and one are the first two factors. From these two, all creation exists, because every number after that is another entity with another quality expressed as quantity or vice versa. And what is an

18

entity? An entity is just another whole, or another one. Just ask the computer.

—

Numbers are a quantilogical way of looking at existence. Qualities expressed as quantities. Each number reaffirms, in its own way, the existence of the zero, like an electron orbiting the nucleus reaffirming the existence of the force that keeps it from being flung into space.

—

One represents unity, the unifying force of the Zero, for it is the Zero that holds together the atoms of the One and each entity thereafter. Each number is a new entity, a new type of one, and this creation is in a way binary. 0's and 1's, like creation on the computer.

—

Light and darkness are not equal. Light is self sustaining. Darkness must hide from it. Light and darkness cannot exist in the same place without darkness' departure. If goodness is light and evil is darkness, then I am encouraged.

—

Nothing is everything. Think about it.

—

The most effective thing that you can do if you are really concerned about the cost of health care is to be healthy so that you don't need it.

—

When we examine ourselves, when we take a look at our lives, we are using our consciousness to examine our consciousness. When we self-examine, it is often difficult to tell the difference between the observer and the observed. Like a mirror examining another mirror.

—

At first glance, it would seem that light and darkness, goodness and evil are equal. But, that isn't really true. Darkness IS an absence of light, but light is self sustaining. Light is eternal and goes on forever. Physics tells us that.

Darkness can only exist where there is a barrier. Darkness must hide from light for its survival.

If good is light and evil is dark, then I am encouraged, because evil's days are numbered…maybe not in my lifetime or maybe so, but evil is not eternal. Goodness is. All that goodness must do is be what it is and increase. Evil's days are numbered. Its time is finite. Evil must hide from good, for evil will not last forever.

—

Before the beginning, there was. For whatever reason, that IS created a symbol to represent itself. That action created duality. Which needed another symbol to represent it, which created a trinity, etc, etc, etc…

—

Before the beginning, there was…

—

The universe is expanding. It has to. Creation is always expanding it. I mean, look how Magic Johnson expanded just the game of basketball. He gave us the high five, the ally-oop, the no-look pass. Yes, the universe is expanding.

—

Every revolving circle is proof of a zero at the center of that circle making its revolution possible. All balance is proof of a zero point making its balance possible.

—

To be centered, one must move beyond emotion. Emotion is energy in motion and has purpose, but motion is not a characteristic of the center. The characteristic of the center is clarity.

—

If the eternal truth were on the tip of your nose and you were making a trip to Tibet to find it, then the trip to Tibet could be a hinderance to your success.

The truth we seek is actually closer than that. We are literally composed of it. The way to truth is inward, not outward.

—

0, 1, 2 - The components of the trinity

H_2O - Two atoms of hydrogen and one atom of oxygen revolving around a zero in the center of the atom….hmmmmmm

—

Art is the use of tangible things to make us feel the intangible.

—

Nothing/Everything = Neverything
(I did not make that up, but I like it!)

—

Nothing exists

—

It is much more important to be a good person than it is a to be a good musician.

—

Every adult should know how to talk with children and how to treat animals. How one interacts with both tells much about the person.

—

This life is the only life we know but not the only life there is.

—

One is the king of all numbers, because all numbers are an entity and therefore a one of some kind. One is the king of all things. All things, though they may have many components, are ultimately one. For one to be one, it needs zero to hold it together. Zero is not a thing, but it is what makes all things, all entities, all ones possible.

—

One is zero made manifest. In all things we see the cohesive property of zero. One has a chance to be itself, because Zero exists and holds all of its parts in place.

—

One is never just one, because zero precedes it. One is zero first. One is zero simultaneously. Keep in mind that there are many numbers between zero and one. Much of Infinity exists between one and zero. If you realize that all things are one, then you see that ALL of creation exists between these two numbers, zero and one.

Just ask the computer.

———

The Father, the Son, the Holy Spirit
The Cohesive manifest is the One
The Balance manifest is the Two
(because zero and oneness are balanced in all things)
The Essence that flows between the manifest and unmanifest, the Holy Spirit, which flows back and forth, in and out of existence.

———

Everything specific represents something not specific. Notes represent music, but music is essence. The essence has a less specific quality. (Joy, passion, love, etc...) That quality is less specific (good, bad, etc...), but ultimately is just an example of the fact that we are alive, that life exists, that the Zero , the "Neverything" is doing its thing.

———

Learn to look past specifics to see the essence.

———

Helen Keller is a great example that the benevolent Zero is present in every circumstance.

———

There is a great analogy in the fact that the center of our solar system is white, life-giving light.

———

Everything that revolves is proof of the zero, because every circle has its center. Everything balanced is proof of the zero, because zero is its balancing point. Everything linear is proof of the zero, because all lines start from there.

———

When you want to change your life, concentrate on the desired essence. Focus there and let the specifics take care of themselves. Focus and pay attention.

———

Humility is a prerequisite of true greatness, because unless one sees his connection to others, his or her achievement or achievements are self centered.

———

To be truly great, one must also be humble. Without humility one's achievements are too easily self centered. If we don't know that we are connected to others, our accomplishments seem as if they have happened for and by ourselves. Humility is the hallmark of greatness.

———

Why be concerned with the state of health care if you don't care enough about the state of your health?

———

If your life ended today, how would you feel about the life you have lived so far?

———

When you look at your divorce in hindsight, eventually you realize that your divorce was not only inevitable but necessary.

—

Every good book involves a page turn.

—

Count Basie said, "It don't mean a thing if it ain't got that swing." I say, "If you can't feel it, conceal it."

—

You've got to hang in there until the sunshines…
From the heartbeat…to the flatline…

—

Don't hate your trials and tribulations
    They ain't nothing but the test of us
And if you can't smile through your frustrations
    Well it happens to the best of us
'Cause nobody knows what you been through
    No one understands, no one but you
And alone ain't lonely when there's
    Strength from above
All there is love
    And the lessons thereof

—

Zero is nothing, but everything
Zero is where it begins
Zero is where it ends
You can't tax a man that has nothing

Zero is freedom or bondage depending on your mindset
Zero is the essence that makes something out of anything…
　　Or nothing…

———

You can hear the notes, but you can't touch the music.

———

Love can be many things
　　Love has so many forms
It can be a fist fight in your defense
　　Or the sun that keeps you warm
Love comes from the heart
　　From your heart comes your passion
But passion needs guidance
　　In some form or fashion
Love needs your heart
　　Your heart needs your mind
Love needs direction
　　So that love isn't blind
Love is the water
　　When a man has thirst
Understanding is the thinking
　　That he may need a cup first
Love is everything
　　So many things that love is for
It can be a mother and her baby
　　Or the reason that we go to war
So let's respect everybody's love
　　Nothing means more than this
Let's always think while we're feeling
　　So that we can co-exist

———

The pen is my sword
    The paper's my shield
The words are my bullets
    But there's nobody killed
I'm not an AK47
    But a weapon of truth
I'm learning from the elderly
    And teaching the youth
I'm a Songwriter!

—

Character speaks on your behalf long before your actions do.
Have character before you write or play music, and it makes your
music better. Wooten Woods was primarily volunteer built, NOT just
because Victor is a good bass player.

I have been to a few funerals and have seen how the character of
a person matters.

—

Martin Luther King
    He did have a dream
Where everyone could live together and
    Love would be redeemed
We shall overcome
    We will live as one
To fan the flames of righteousness
    Until the day is won

—

Everyday we start from scratch
    Like an egg that's about to hatch
Like a bully that's met his match
    Like a cold we're about to catch

Everyday we are reborn
    When the sun comes in the morn
When the lessons have been learned
    And the nighttime has adjourned

Everyday brings the dawn
    And time keeps marching on
And this moment here, that we hold so dear
    Tomorrow will be gone

Everyday will be tomorrow
    And whether it's joy or sorrow
Depends on you, what you think or do
    And there's no time that we can borrow

Everyday is yesterday
    When tomorrow comes its way
The past is under lock and latch
    Everyday we start from scratch

———

A "problem child" represents at least one adult who has let them down, and if we take the arts from them we have let them down.

———

If life without the arts is unthinkable, how can it be that education without the arts is the solution?

———

Technology is simultaneously a step forward and a step backward.

———

Someone asked me, "Do you want the best for the person you love even if what is best for them doesn't include you?"

—

The past will stay in the past if you let go of it.

—

Behind every criticism is a voice saying, "If only they were more like me."

—

Brutal honesty is still brutality.

—

With your wife, girlfriend, or significant other…
Sometimes winning ain't winning.

—

Time being finite, is a tool. And like all tools, it is meant to be put down after its use has been fulfilled.

—

When we are young we can't wait to get older.
When we get older we long for our youth.
When we are at work, we can't wait for the weekend.
We long for graduation while in high school or college and reminisce about our carefree, bill-free, school days once we get a job.
One day we get old and wonder where all the time went.
Most of it was spent wishing we were somewhere else.

—

Being a true winner has very little to do with the score.

—

Is there any joy greater than knowing your young ones are doing well?

—

Every teacher has much more of a responsibility to reach down to a young student than the youngster has to reach up to the teacher.

—

Pain is life's way of letting you know without a doubt that something is wrong.

—

No man is an island, but we ARE individuals.

—

If you want me to stay then let me be free.
If you want me to leave then confine me.

—

To inspire a young person for the better, to positively impact the life of a child, brings a satisfaction that no award on Earth can match.

—

At the worst times of my life, I have always had music. My worst times have always been bearable.

—

A great teacher not only should have a high skill level but should also have the ability to make that skill level appear attainable to the student.

—

The Fourth Amendment and its right to privacy was written long before nuclear weapons. I understand all sides of the right to privacy argument.

—

Life, no one gets out alive.

—

When they invented the automobile, I am sure the horse breeders were not happy.

—

Every generation has old people who complain about how good things used to be and how things have changed for the worst. I don't want to be a new old guy who disguises a fear of change with a love of the "good old days".

—

If you do not take the time to be smart, someone else will make your important decisions for you. Intelligence is true power.

—

Ignorance more than malice is too often our worst problem. I mean, if you go to Asia and you call a Korean person Japanese or

Chinese by mistake, you may have a problem…NOT because you hate Asians but because of your ignorance of ethnicity.

—

If you want Peace, start by being peaceful.

—

I hope that I have set a good enough example for my kids.

—

When trying to live a life of quality, it is easy to be too hard on yourself.

—

Where is the line between doing what comes natural and having self control?

—

Life teaches all the time. Pay attention!

—

We are the truth that we seek. We are akin to a numeral not only striving to understand its uniqueness but also striving to understand the zero that precedes it and all numbers. The study of self is both a study of individualism and universal connectedness.

—

Words, the double-edged sword…

—

Laughter in life is like recess from a tough class.

—

Apathy is often the coward's way of not taking a side or taking a stand.

—

Cynicism is the intellect's way of trying to discredit the heart, point by point.

—

The heart, as impractical as it can often be, is infinitely necessary and the center of our spirituality or lack thereof.

—

When we rode horses for travel, we could smell the flowers. We knew what was in bloom. We appreciated the foliage and the comfort of a gentle breeze.
With the invention of the automobile, most of that was lost. With the airplane, most if not all of the appreciation was gone too.
Technology is a step forward and a step backward. It not only shortens the process but eliminates the benefits of the process.

—

The future is not here yet, and the past is gone.

—

Bless this food that it helps to keep our bodies strong, our minds clear, and our hearts pure.
Amen.

—

You can't negotiate a contract with your heart, and you can't hug someone with your intellect...not effectively anyway.

—

Problems are just solutions in disguise the same way that 2+2=4. The problem is equal to the solution.

—

A problem is the same as the solution except for the fact that a problem involves a process.

—

Space is never empty. The zero is always there.

—

Nothing means "no thing", and where there are no things there is still existence.

—

If I had to do it all over again ...I would probably say, "Dang!"

—

It is hard to be an effective driver if you have too much attention on the rear view mirror.

—

No time is the perfect time in this imperfect world. (But keep in mind that nothing is everything.)

—

A mother who lives long enough to see her child reach the end of his or her life will never be quite the same again. My mother wasn't.

—

The down side of the intellect is that it often obscures the obvious when there is something that it doesn't want to see.

—

All things in life are neutral. Meaning comes from us. We are what give things their meaning and their context.

—

The heart gives us a broad feel for the essence of life as we perceive it to be. The mind, or the intellect, gives us a precise view of the perceived life's details. Neither the heart nor the mind is any more accurate than the other because they are flip sides of the same coin of perception.

—

Joy is a wonderful feeling that diminishes the moment you try to put it into words.
Pain is a sensation that worsens the more you put it into words.

—

An optimist sees a world of opportunity that supports his/her positive outlook. A pessimist looks out and sees a world that supports his/her dark outlook.

—

Silence can be more enjoyable than your favorite song.

—

The world is more technologically connected and less personally connected.

—

A bad day playing music is better than a good day of doing a looooot of things!

—

The intellect has its place. Sometimes we do need specifics, statistics, details, and precision. One cannot do their taxes with tarot cards.

—

I have self confidence, because I believe what I have to say about me more than I believe what you have to say about me. I do think highly of myself. Thanks, Mom!

—

Self confidence is not the same as arrogance.

—

Society suffers when the news meant to inform us descends into entertainment with current events.

—

A school teacher does not get nearly the credit or the pay that he or she deserves.

—

The person who complains about the low pay of school teachers in one breath and fights for the lowering of his taxes may as well quit talking.

—

Many people are not motivated one way or the other. Many are sitting on the fence, in the middle, waiting for the next big tide to sway them one way or the other.

—

I believe in the goodness of people. I think that most people are better than they think they are. People are at their best when things are worst and too often at their worst when they are comfortable.

—

What many people see as "luck" is often just an unexpected result of preparation. A golfer gets a "hole in one" because he/she has prepared for years to hit the ball close to the hole. I am "lucky" to live the life I live as a musician, but I worked hard to get here.

—

There is a reason why great shooters in basketball get more "lucky" bounces than you.

—

It is equally, if not more important, for you to be as smart as you are talented.

—

There is nothing that makes a woman more beautiful to me than her being intelligent.

—

Love does not always mean relationship.

—

It makes no sense that most doctors are novices of nutrition.

—

Fear always lurks in the shadows. It feels self sufficient but needs our energy for its survival.

—

Never be ashamed even if what they say about you is true.

—

An open mind should balance a principled one.

—

Victory rewards. Losing teaches. Loss is not losing if you learn and get better. Losing does not have to be defeat. In fact, losing and its lessons are integral stepping stones to future victory.

—

A person who cannot lose with dignity is not fit to win. Character is always more important than outcome.

—

Show me someone who is never wrong and I will show you an unmarried person with no friends.

—

For the people wanting to spread religion, there needs to be more convincing examples than the 40 day flood, the talking snake, and the burning bush.

—

Arguing with crazy makes you both look insane.

—

Apathy is often the intellect's way of dealing with matters of the heart. The heart or the head is a choice, and when we don't want to feel what is in our heart we too often choose apathy, the intellect's attempt to give you an intelligent reason to not do or feel anything.

—

Honesty can be used as a weapon, and the truth can be used for brutality.

—

A woman is beautiful in so many ways. Every woman is beautiful in some way.

—

Love is what you feel. A relationship is what you do.

—

Some have trouble putting their feelings into words. Some have trouble listening with their heart as well as their ears. Yet, communication must still occur.

—

Zero is everywhere...One is its messenger...

—

I read somewhere that an extreme optimist is like a person who while falling off of a building says, "At least we have not hit the ground yet..."

—

I read somewhere that anger is like picking up a red hot coal with the intention of throwing it at someone.

—

I would love to be as good of a human being as my dog thinks that I am.

—

Life! No one gets out alive.

—

Our bodies are living symbols of what we are and who we think we are.

—

Ask yourself who you are and watch your answer change.

—

Trying to put the goodness of life into words is sometimes like talking through a good concert, trying to explain what you like about the music. Shhhh…!

—

One enables zero to be everywhere, for without One there is nowhere.

—

One cannot always pre-think their path to success. You need clarity, not to design the path, but to be fully cognizant and prepared to recognize it when you see it…to hold in your heart the essence of what you want and let the details come as they may.

—

The doodoo exiting your butt is as important to this life as the ideas entering your mind.

—

The pentatonic scale at one time was known as the "slave scale", the scale heard coming from the voices of the slaves in the belly of the ship during the slave trade.
The "blues scale", in my opinion, was the scale of the former slave still struggling in America telling his story.
Funk Music, the child of rhythm and blues, to me is the music of the self aware free Black man with "Soul Power", thanking life "Falettin me be mice elf agin". Funk is not so much about the struggle but more bout the celebration. Funk is rhythmic dignity.

—

Without rhythm, music is just a pile of notes.

—

Always listen to the elderly.

—

Always listen to children.

—

Always listen.
    Focus and clarity must precede effective actions and successful undertakings.

—

Sometimes there are no good options.

—

In music the rests are as important as the notes.

—

    I want my music to reach the masses, to inspire the right way…like a clear eyed Sly Stone/Stevie Wonder.

—

    The feeling of hopelessness is often the feeling of worthlessness covered up.

—

A woman is a man's sexual kite in intimacy. Why do we enjoy kites? Because kites can go to heights that we can never get to. It's height is a symbol of our kite flying skill. The higher it goes, the more it shows just how skilled we are...as kite flyers.

In intimacy, a woman's level of arousal has no limits. A man's arousal potential is more limited, since it is "land locked" to his orgasm. A woman's arousal is potentially limitless and her height of excitement and arousal is testament to a man's "skill", how "good" he is at what he does. A woman is not bound by her orgasm and can soar to places a man cannot go.

Some days are tougher than others to get your kite in the air. Some days the wind is just not right. No kite will fly well if you only concentrate on the controls in your hand. There is no limit to the amount of string if you pay close attention to how the kite moves in the air. A well cared for kite might fly even higher next time.

There is nothing like the sight of a beautiful kite in the air.

———

I love my home, but if I am locked in, if I cannot come and go as I please, then my home that I love becomes a prison.

———

I don't like the idea of trading my privacy for my safety. I value my privacy. But there are people who want to kill as many people as possible, and the idea of them with their privacy is dangerous to us all.

———

We are mirrors of our Creator, like every number fully contains the zero that gave it birth. And like mirrors, when we are aligned with our source, the reflections are infinite and it becomes difficult to differentiate the Creator from the created, the reflector from the reflected.

43

—

I don't want to run the world. I just want to change it for the better.

—

Nothing is more powerful than the power of positive example.

—

Love is more than can be put into words.

—

Sometimes you just don't know what to say. At those times it is probably best to say nothing.

—

The only difference from here to there is the time it takes to get from here to there.

—

The nature of existence is circular, the circle of life, "what goes around comes around", the zero, etc.

The nature of matter is square, i.e. a square meal, the shape of an acre of land, a man with no soul is "square", etc. Yet, the square and the circle should exist in balance since both are 360 degrees.

—

Your legacy is not entirely up to you, because it depends largely upon opportunity, and opportunity is not up to you. What you bring to potential opportunity IS up to you.

—

Success does not come from just getting what you want. It comes from, first, recognizing opportunity and then making the most of what's given.

—

People are destroyed more by getting what they want than they are by failure.

—

Talent is a potential, like an acorn is a potential tree. It is hard to hang a tree swing on an acorn.

—

Success is not so much meeting your goals. Success is obtained by the qualities gained when you set a goal. Success is obtained by a combination of focus, clarity, and the recognition of opportunities.

—

It is important to set a goal, to get from point A to point B. Success is gained not so much from getting to point B. No one can predict the future. Chances are, your destination will be different than what you planned. But if you set a goal and strive for it, it will take clarity, focus, perseverance, etc. With clarity you will recognize new opportunity when it arrives. With focus you will hone whatever skill it takes to meet the opportunity, and perseverance will give you the endurance to follow through. Always set goals, but do not be stubborn if the goal changes. Tunnel vision blocks much needed peripheral views that are necessary for success.

—

Success has as much to do with who you become as what you accomplish. Maybe more...

—

Communication has as much to do with listening as it does with speaking your mind.

—

The sting of an inferior product lasts much longer than the thrill of the bargain.

—

Vulnerability is a recipe for growth.

—

The most dangerous racist is not the nazi, skinhead, or the KKK member. The most dangerous racist is the racist that does not know he/she is a racist.

—

Most of the wisdom that comes out of our mouths are truths that pertain to us. We often teach the lessons that we most need to learn.

—

A young musician needs a responsible adult to prepare that musician for the day when his/her age is not an attraction...or a factor.

—

If your parent has an issue, like alcohol, drug addiction, violence, etc., the child is likely to either become the same problem or overcome the same problem, but one way or another, they are likely to encounter the same issues as they become adults.

—

Do not be afraid of defeat because it is your greatest mentor if you are ever to know victory.

—

Victory, as sweet as it is, is more reward than teacher and often more of a robber of character than defeat.

—

When there is controversy, agreement is not often possible. As human points of view, we cannot concur on everything. What is not only possible but necessary, is for us all to be able to understand viewpoints that are not our own even when we don't agree. It is imperative if we have any hope of moving forward as a society. In issues of race, we need to be able to understand the context of opposing views and not be so laser focused on our issues that we forget that there are other races besides black and white. There are issues of gender, sexual orientation, religion, etc. Let's keep our minds open and remember that being "right" is not enough.

—

Young people will make this world a better place if we adults don't corrupt them with bad example.

—

Every time you see a sunrise, keep in mind that there is one less that you get a chance to see.

—

If Ann Frank can believe in the goodness of people, so can I.

—

We want our elected officials to do certain things, but as citizens we have responsibilities too. We also need to "reach across the aisle" and find common ground and the ability to communicate without tearing down. Why should we expect from our leaders qualities that we do not exhibit?

—

Good will is at its best when it is not only expressed here and there. Christmas shows us how we should be all the time. We are good people, but let's be better.

—

If I am a good man, keep in mind that great men come from great men. My Dad was quiet, but he was strong and steady. Those are qualities that you don't recognize as a kid so much. You tend to take them for granted. He was there everyday, every gig, and would not let us even mow the grass so that we could stay focused on what he knew was our calling. THAT is a father. We did not thank him as kids with words. We did not know to. He just kept giving us what we needed long after we had graduated high school, and other friends and relatives, I am sure, were urging him to have us move on and get "real jobs".

A mother's worth is easier to see. Mom's get the credit that the deserve, and they DO deserve it. But a good dad's worth is often harder to see.

So, out loud, I say, "Thanks, Dad!". Your strength and steadiness have given me quite a life!

—

Muhammad Ali was as big an influence on me as any musician.

—

Anytime you mention Muhammad Ali you silently mention Joe Frazier at the same time.

—

I feel like I am on the edge of something great.
    July 21, 2013
    McClean, Virginia

—

People who excuse their dietary habits with the idea of, "Well, you have to die of something…" often, when they start to die of something, are the first in line at Whole Foods or GNC.

—

Everyday is one day closer to my final tomorrow.

—

It is much more important what kind of person you become than how well you learn to play your instrument.

—

"Nothing", no thing, is not synonymous with non existence.

—

Everything starts from nothing. Nothing gives birth to everything. Remember the center of the globe where literally 0 is 100%.

—

Re-examine the phrase, "I have nothing." When you think about it, that phrase can be a statement of profound power, not of lack.

—

What is it that turns nothing into something? Now, THAT is a question worth taking a look at. Creativity turns nothing into something. Creativity makes something out of nothing. It is like a magic potion bestowed upon us out of nowhere.

—

The Zero is unmanifest creativity.

—

Creativity is an intangible that comes from intelligence.

—

Success is destructive when you get to your goal but did not gain character on the way.

—

Why is it that the only things that we put to the taste test are foods meant to be good for us? No one ever says that they won't take liquid Tylenol or Robitussin because it tastes badly.

—

"Not Guilty" is not the same as innocent.

—

Most people would do better if they knew better.

—

Matter is manifested nothingness. It has only the meaning that we give it.

—

True vision has little to do with your eyes.

—

Some things don't need questioning. Questions are always a product of the intellect which often arrogantly thinks that its precise point by point examination of life makes it much more qualified than the heart.
Ask the question, "What is happiness?" and you have already gotten in its way.

—

When you evaluate something by its worst attribute, it says more about you than whatever you are describing harshly.

—

Perception is more choice than it is fact.

—

A flower is beauty that you can see. Music, is beauty that you can hear. Both have beauty you can feel.

—

The Funk is not the
    Baby shower on the agenda
It's the blood & the mucus
    Of the baby placenta
It may not be the baby
    With the bow in her hair
Funk is the reason
    That the baby is there

—

The things that we are most sure of are the things we don't mention much. Be careful of the declarations that you make repeatedly for they too often broadcast your insecurities.

—

It is always important to have balance, and the higher you rise, the more important it becomes.

—

Everything visible represents something invisible.

—

Chaos is an attempt to live without the zero, without a center.

—

Success without the necessary character gained from the journey of its acquisition always leads to failure or destruction.

—

A circle is only as good as the quality of its center. You are the center of your circle of events. Think about that.

—

Creation is an intangible that makes the most out of all the other factors of life.

—

Zero is the center of life. It's function is creativity. We are the center of our own lives too, and our function should also be creativity.

—

Part of life is like a well written symphony. The sunrises and sunsets, the movement of the seasons, the ebb and flow of the tide. The fun parts are improvisation.

—

Being a great musician has less to do with what you play and more to do with why you played it, especially when it involves improvising.

—

We are always teaching whether we know it or not. What are you teaching? What is it that you are an example of?

—

Your body is less like a machine and more like an ecosystem. It is up to us to keep our ecosystems in balance.

—

Balance, as important as it is, is a tool, a tool to help us get back to Oneness. Balance is the highest offering of the number 2. Its duality is there to teach us Oneness. Oneness is the highest calling of manifestation. Its function is to make the Zero manifest.

—

Creation is the Father, the Son, and the Holy Spirit or the Unmanifest, the Manifest, and the Creativity.

—

Sexuality is much more between the ears than it is between the legs.

—

Duality is the teacher. Balance is the lesson. Oneness is the goal.

—

It is not arrogant to know your true power or the extent of your inner beauty or outer beauty for that matter. Arrogance is dependent upon how you handle it.

—

Am I extraordinarily special and valuable? Yes!
Am I worth more than anyone else? No!
How you answer that second question determines whether it is self worth, self confidence, or arrogance.

—

Positive qualities are too often diminished by words and increased by experience. Love, Happiness, Friendship, Trust, etc... Negative qualities are increased by words and experience. Sadness, loneliness, hate, etc. Sometimes we just talk too much!

—

One who is a great communicator must also know the value of silence and listening.

—

Communication is more than just making a good point or merely telling the truth. To truly communicate, one needs good instincts about the mindset of the listener. You also need good instincts about your mindset AS a listener.

—

In life, think of yourself as a talented rookie athlete. What are the mistakes rookies make? Apply that to life.

—

Life is always giving answers to those that listen.

—

Those of us who are considered enlightened are no closer to perfection than those considered un-enlightened, so don't be so judgmental.

—

Devil never even lived. (Palindrome)

—

Doctors tell you all they know, but that doesn't mean that's all there is.

—

Your health is your own responsibility.

—

Creativity can be for the creative person one of the greatest reasons to procrastinate.

—

Character is a refinement of personality and morals. To be a "character" is to be a personality without refinement and morals.

—

I think nature knows what it is doing.

—

When you are in puberty, it is very easy for your genitals to write their own instructions. Adults too...

—

When I was young, I remember having lots of fantasies, but I don't remember any of them containing a condom.

—

Love is more than emotion. Some love is not emotional.

—

Knowing is not enough if it is not followed by action.

—

Life is One thing that plays out in a lot of different ways.

—

One is either the loneliest number or the most powerful, depending upon the perspective you choose. It can represent isolation or all-inclusiveness.

—

In the sense that all things are specific entities, everything is some type of one. In my opinion, One is not the loneliest number. One is the "onliest" number that encompasses all of Creation.

—

Sometimes there are no good choices. It is not always a choice between bad and good. Sometimes the choice is between bad and worse.

—

Sometimes anger is appropriate. Do all you can to avoid it.

—

People, too often, don't realize how they help themselves or get in their own way simply by being who they are.

—

If you are not the same people as you were when you got married, and you don't get along or see eye to eye anymore, then you owe it to each other to move on, especially if you have kids. You owe them a good example.

To have a career as a musician requires more than just being talented.

—

I have heard it said more than once that "Hope is not a plan." That is true. Hope is not a plan, but it IS the prerequisite to any plan that has any chance of success. Any plan without hope is pointless.

—

Sometimes we are friends with people who are not good for us just because we are so familiar with them. We have known them for so long. Even when they treat us badly, we are reluctant to let them go because of our long history. We love them even though we know they mistreat us.

For many of us, our long standing illnesses are very similar to these friends, and we are reluctant to make the necessary changes for the better because of our history and our embrace of the familiar.

—

If we love nature, why do we hate pornography?

—

Emotional love for someone, often but not always, has as much or more to do with how that person "makes us feel" than it is concerned with what is best for the person of interest. Pepe Le Pew is totally "in love", but his "love" has no regard for his "lover's" feelings or well being. His heart has made the decision for her. Don't let your "love" be a type of emotional self pleasure. Emotion is "energy in motion", and motion is never centered, (since the center never moves). Emotion is dual, up and down. At best, emotional love is exciting, exhilarating, and intoxicating. At worst, it is needy and

unreasonable. Love for our lover rises and falls, comes and goes. We love our lovers "because..."
We don't love our children "because..."
We just love them.

—

To be loved by many can be both flattering and confining.

—

Words are empty unless people give them substance.

—

Do not be so mindful of the needs of others that you do not care for yourself equally as much. Self neglect is not a virtue.

—

It is not arrogance to know you are priceless. It is arrogance to think you are more priceless than another.

—

One is the tool of the Zero. Zero provides the cohesiveness of existence and One carries out its actions.

—

The realization that you cannot be there for everyone in need is sobering. We cannot be everything to everybody, and that is easiest to understand when we are not the ones wanting the help.

—

Nutrition is every bit as much of a religious practice as my "religion". I am as vigilant of what I put in my body as I am with the thoughts and beliefs of my heart and mind. How can they be separate?

—

What good is it to know the laws of the spirit but be a novice of the laws of nutrition?

—

An "expert" of the afterlife but a novice of the present life…hmmmm….

—

Embrace your hardships for they are great teachers. Our struggles teach us and provide much needed lessons. Who can truly and realistically desire wisdom while rejecting the lessons that potentially could provide it?

—

Can a light bulb complain of a dark room? Can a diamond complain of not having money? Can a fish complain of thirst or a gust of wind complain of suffocation? All that we want in life we embody. And we must realize that first before we can experience it in our outward lives.

—

What we need in life is there. What we want often is not. No problem comes without a solution, but we have to be more vigilant for the answer than we are disappointed that we did not get what we wanted or asked for.

—

Business does not always operate without emotion, but to be effective, it must have that capacity.

—

Physical health is as important as mental health. One enhances the other for they are flip sides of the same coin.

—

The past is written in pen.
The present is written is pencil.
The future is not written yet.
You are the writing utensil.
Time is the paper.

—

Never make one an enemy for the purpose of testing their friendship. Friendships, though more durable than love affairs, are fallible also.

—

Not wanting to hurt anyone becomes more difficult when you put yourself on that list.

—

The health of your whole body largely is a testament to the health of your intestines.

—

For the happiness that you need to come to you, you cannot keep insisting that the happiness you want looks like what you want it to or fits your specifications.

———

The downside of rising to new heights is that you lose some of the beauty of detail of your connection with the ground.

———

To try to be everything to everyone often results in you being very little to those same people.

———

What is best for others cannot be at your expense.

———

When you loosen your grasp, you have more of an opportunity for other things to enter your hand. What we need in life, a lot of it, is not in our field of vision. So learn and let go.

———

Careful or carefree. Choose carefully.

———

Even when you love them all, you can't love all of them.

———

It is easier to complain than it is to change.

———

Part of life is given, and part of it is up to you. Wisdom is knowing the difference.

—

Do what you must do and let the rest take care of itself.

—

True greatness starts with humility in the same manner that the largest numbers possible start with zero. "Greatness" without humility is merely arrogance. True greatness without humility is impossible.

—

To truly know is beyond learning. A spider does not learn to spin a web.

—

To be and to do are separate things. One is dependent upon the other but not vice versa.

—

Don't hate your
    Trials and tribulations
They ain't nothin' but
    The test of us
And if you can't smile
    Through your frustrations
Well it happens to
    The best of us
'Cause nobody knows what
    You've been through

No one understands
    No one but you
And alone ain't lonely when
    There's faith from above
All there is a Love
    And the lessons thereof

—

Faith from above is really faith from within.

—

Humor is valuable because it gives our spirit freedom from the tyranny of circumstance and direct access to some joy even in the worst of situations.

—

Life is existence. Life's awareness that it is alive…is consciousness.

—

Perception is a type of seeing, but it is not the same as vision. Perception is a tool of learning that "sees" based on what it believes. We perceive someone to be an enemy until we learn they are a friend. A child perceives the Boogie Man is under his bed. Perception is at its   worst when it is confused with vision.

—

What we are precedes who we are. The fact that we are is beyond discussion.

—

So much of the goodness of life is not specific. Words and concepts are specific. Beware of trying to verbalize and conceptualize existence, because their specificity is often at the expense of the very thing they are trying to examine.

—

Knowing does not require action. The center of the circle does not do anything. It just IS, and that makes all doing possible.

—

Cynicism is the opposite of inspiration, because it looks at life in its worst possible terms in a feeble attempt to "keep it real". Where the average person sees a beautiful dog, the cynic sees an animal with bad breath, that poops all the time, that may bite you, and sheds, thereby worsening your allergies.

—

Talk, but don't talk too much.

—

Think, but don't think too much.

—

What good is wisdom if it is not put into practice?

—

The intellect can use "why" as an educated reason NOT to do what it knows needs to be done.

—

Life is at its best when acceptance replaces wishes and hopes.

—

Relentless generosity is not always the answer.

—

When you get what you ask for, it does not always feel like you thought it would.

—

Death is nothing but Life on the day that the caterpillar becomes the butterfly.

—

If you think this life is an illusion, then hold your breath and let me know what happens.

—

We don't always understand the "why" of it, but it is our responsibility to understand the "what" of it and see situations for what they are, even when we don't know why they happen.

—

You cannot punish a young person into being a good kid.

—

We, too often, are in fear of the dark more than we are comfortable in the light.

—

If the Truth that we seek was on the tip of our nose, then there would be no need to go out and seek it. The journey outward could be a hinderance. Well, the truth of the matter is that the truth is even closer than that. We ARE the truth, and the outward search helps us miss the point.

—

Beware of becoming too connected or dependent upon technology, because ultimately your life will come down to who you are, what you believe, what you stand for. Technology is good in that it helps us to be more efficient by eliminating the process. It can be to our detriment when it blocks the benefits of the process. One who is internet dependent will never fully be self sufficient, because you will always be dependent upon those who take care of the internet. The internet and technology have allowed me to learn much about nutrition. My mother could grow her own crops and had stores of home grown food "just in case". Who would you say is better off?

—

I have heard it said more than once that "we should hope for the best and prepare for the worst." I have a different take on that theory.

In life we have a tendency to see the world in the context of our mindset. Ask any mother about when she was pregnant and how the world at that time seemed to be all about babies. Think about every "sweet" person that we know. They all have "dear dear friends" or other "sweet" friends. Or think about the person in a bad mood who thinks the world is full of "ass holes". A thief sees a world of people who may want to steal from him/her. We see the world in the context of our mindset.

So let's go back to "preparing for the worst" and "hoping for the best". In my opinion, the error is that we "believe" in evil and we "hope" for good. We have faith in the power of evil and "hooooope" that goodness will have influence. In my opinion, goodness has as much power or more than evil. Evil flourishes because of the fact that even though we hate it, we honor it. Goodness is a dream that we HOPE comes true, while evil is something to prepare for NOW.

So what do we do? I think, instead of preparing for the worst, we should strive to be our best. We should strive to have character, to be prepared, to honor each other. If we are at our best, then we ARE prepared for the worst without having to see the world in its worst context first.

A police officer or a person in charge of homeland security has to prepare for the worst. He or she does not have the opportunity to assume that people will behave as they should. But we are not beings that have to constantly be on guard or assume that someone is planning on robbing or taking advantage of us. Let's be at our best, see the world in its best light, and know that IF we are at our best, when the worst happens we will be ready.

In summation, I think if we are at our best, we WILL be ready for the worst while being able to enjoy the best of what life has to offer. Prepare for the best as much as you prepare for the worst and you are at your best. Expect the best from people and often they live up to your expectations. Expect the worst, and often that is what we get. But remember, it starts with us.

From the blog, "Hope, and Preparing For The Worst"
        September 26, 2013

——

When we feel limitation from within, we then often create an imaginary external limitation.

——

If you are not going to use medication, then you must substitute it with dedication of nutrition.

——

Everyone's personality comes in a shape that has some holes in it.

—

Funk is the descendant of the blues. The blues says, "Nobody loves me but my mother, and she might be jiving too." Funk is the music risen from adversity, thanking life for letting it be itself, again…again as in remembering that it was once free, reclaiming freedom. Funk is the benefactor of the blues, standing atop the winner's podium with a raised clenched fist in defiance and inclusiveness.

—

Funk is the sex before the conception, the amniotic fluid, the mucus plug, and the water breaking. Funk is the dirt before the vegetable, the labor pain before the birth. Funk is the Alpha and Omega, because we start from the dirt and return to the dirt. Funk is the teacher and the lessons before the blessin'.

—

The truer we get, the more similar we become.

—

If you feel powerless, you either have to accept the fact that you are powerless or find a way to feel powerful.

—

As far as I am concerned, the stuff that means the most to me is the stuff we don't have to say.

—

I won't say that it's not a perfect world, but I will say that this is not a world tailored to your expectations.

—

Why is it that we seldom look at a person doing the right thing and say, "Look at what this world is coming to."

—

If you can't back the team when they are losing, you don't deserve to celebrate with them when they win.

—

You never know the extent of your influence on people by being who you are supposed to be.

—

The context of your life is much more important than the contents of your life if you want to be happy.

—

The only difference in the single electron of an atom of hydrogen and a dangerous free radical is that the hydrogen electron has context to the zero point at the center of the atom and the free radical exists without context and is therefore potentially destructive.

Order or disorder, construction or destruction is dependent upon the context of the contents and not just the contents alone.

—

If you want stability in your life, start by being stable.

—

Blaming society is our attempt to blame "us" without having to blame ourselves.

—

My favorite part of travel is not all the things that I get to see. It is the people that I get a chance to meet. I have yet to meet an uninteresting person.

—

In all things, be as centered as possible. Even a hurricane has a calm center.

—

Only in the center are you connected to everything.

—

It is not always a matter of whether or not you are at fault. Sometimes the issue is whether or not you are a player in the dysfunction.

—

Puberty is awkward necessity.

—

A light bulb has no reason to curse the darkness.

—

The secret to happiness is not just forgetting the past or looking forward to the future. Both of those can help, but the real secret of happiness is appreciating the present for all that it has to offer.

———

Happiness is a feeling that we get when we decide to see the parameters of our life in a favorable context.

Many of the things in life that mean the most to us cannot not be taken away.

———

Never fall for the idea that ordinary is not extra ordinary.

———

Learn to see the present in depth.

———

What you get out of life is largely dependent upon what you put into it.

———

Nothing is everywhere.
No thing is everywhere.

———

It is easier to blame someone else for our problems than it is to look at ourselves and admit that we have problems.

———

Real learning is gained by looking inward before looking outward.

—

Even your worst day is a privilege.

—

Talent can get you there. Character keeps you there.

—

Success or the lack thereof is about who you have become, NOT what you have accomplished. Many who have accomplished much still come up short as people.

—

Nothing is everywhere. Nothing is everything. All agree on these points in one way or another.

—

If your life is a mess, first recognize the dynamics of your mess and then arrange them in a way that makes sense. The chromatic scale is a mess before the notes are arranged.

—

Life is a combination of opportunity and will power. One is a gift and one is a choice, but you must be aware enough to recognize the gifts and strong enough to exert your will when necessary.

—

Notes are the tools of music but not the music itself, any more than a pile of wood, hammer, and nails are a house.

Life is what you do with space and parameters.

Do not be fooled by the adoration you receive when you are on the stage. The stage forces people to kook up to you and see you in your best light. Accept the adoration, but maintain your humility and balance, because the truth is that you are not more than they.

Treat people in your life with the same love and respect that you would have for them if you were at their funeral. Do not wait for your friends to be gone before you cherish them.

Emotion is "energy in motion'. It is a very necessary part of life, but it is not a very good decision maker.

Happiness or sadness is not caused by the events of our lives. It is caused by our perception of those events and the context that we see them in. What is loss to one and a descent into despair, is a lesson for another and a stepping stone to better days. Context is to events what space is to notes, what zero is to one.

To be an expert of the afterlife but a novice of the present life makes no sense to me.

To fully realize your power and your worth and not include arrogance is not only important, it is necessary and imperative.

—

As best you can, always nurture the ability to stay calm. In all matters, keep a conscious connection with your center. Clarity resides there.

—

A true teacher inspires his or her students and is inspired by them as well.

—

The person who attempts to count to infinity is no more closer than the person who never started.

—

It often appears to me that the diet of too many religious people will get them to the after life much faster.

—

There is no greater reward than the privilege of knowing that you have inspired a young person for the better.

—

Emotional love must have clarity at its center. Otherwise, it is unbalanced and without rationale.

—

If an artist pays as much attention to their character as their art, then they will be prepared or strong enough to endure the hardships of a career in the music business. When the tough times arrive, it will matter more who you are and what you are made of than how talented you are.

—

Look at the football career of Archie Manning. Now look at Archie's life and try to tell me that he is not a winner.

—

Never let your personality get in the way of your skills.

—

What kind of person are you when things are at their worst? The answer to this question says a lot about your level of character.

—

The only difference between here and there is the time it takes to get from one to the other. Here and there is just a matter of context. I say, "I am here". The ant says your heels are here and your toes are there, far away. Time is a tool to help us separate and examine the parameters of life. Without it, life would be like playing notes of a masterpiece all at the same time.

—

Sometimes you choose and sometimes you are chosen.

—

If life chooses you, it is up to you to go beyond your fear and know that for you to be chosen you must be capable.

—

I don't want to conquer the world, but I do want my life to affect it for the better.

—

Everyone is capable of goodness, but not everyone has the bravery to go against the grain, step away from the crowd, and do good first. There are always more followers than leaders.

—

Passion can be both blessing and curse.

—

When giving to those less fortunate, It is important to remember that you are not reaching down but reaching out to an equal. Do not be benevolently arrogant. Arrogance is improper even when it has a bow on it.

—

True love does not exist for purpose. True love is not a means to an end. Some would say that love is oneness. I would say love is more like the zero that makes one-ness possible.

—

I am not afraid of ghosts. More places are "haunted" by the humans still living than those passed on.

—

There is no such thing as goal oriented friendship.

—

The depth of my friendship is not determined by the number of times that we talk to each other.

—

The war on poverty should be the war against hopelessness. One can overcome poverty if he or she has hopes, but without hope there is no need to strive or overcome. How can we ignite the spark of hope in our young people? The first thing we can do is be the kind of people that we want them to be, and show them by example the value of character.

—

In life there will always come a time when hard times arrive. On that day, it will not matter how well you sing or play. A majority of your life will be spent off of your instrument. Character is more important than talent.

—

Marriage is both love and relationship. Love is how you feel. Relationship is what you do. The two are related but not the same, and it is important to know the difference.

—

Today I am happy, and that feels very good!

—

Between zero and one there is a relationship that facilitates and enables all of creation. In my opinion, that relationship is the Holy

Spirit. Zero is the Father of all creation. One is the Son that makes all other Oneness possible.

—

Do not miss the beauty of the vastness of Life by trying to identify all of its parts.

—

Do not love because...just love.

—

Part of life is bittersweet. There is no way around it.

—

All numbers are finite. They have a start and a finish. When they finish, the zero will remain. Zero is the beginning and the end, the alpha and the omega.

—

We come from zero. We are maintained by the zero. We will return to the zero.

—

Men are simpler beings with very few layers. Women are much more multi-layered. It is unfortunate that, too often, women must be the teachers of men.

—

One thing that is certain about life is that change is inevitable.

Love is hard to describe. It is difficult to accurately define something so vast with these finite words.

———

True love is more than merely a desire to be with someone. The truest love exceeds merely having someone as the object of your affection. True love sometimes must let go of the loved one, because true love is care for another's well being, even when the loved one's destiny or desire for another takes them away from you. Yes, true love is often bittersweet and can test whether your love is really care or just the desire to be with him or her. True love is not a constant embrace. Sometimes it is just the opposite. Sometimes the truest love watches the loved one fade into the distance, confident that the distance will not sever the connection, confident that the change is for the best. True love is selfless. A mother loves her child as much or more than herself, because at one point that child was her own flesh, yet she must let him or her go. Sometimes, the truest love is not in the embrace…it is in the letting go…

———

Life on this Earth is a constant now that is always changing.

———

Clarity gives you vision. Vision gives you the ability to prepare. Preparation enables you to manage change in an orderly fashion…as easy as a right turn that you saw coming while driving. Without clarity, vision, and preparation, that right turn would be destructive.

———

You never know the effect that your character and behavior will have on others, nor its extent. Therefore, do what you can to always be at your best.

—

If you desire success start by being one who deserves it.

—

The subject of change is simultaneously the subject of consistency.

—

At its best, change is nothing more than the appropriate adaptation to a world that ceases to remain the same. At its worst, change is chaos. The difference is that positive change has a core, and chaos has no center.

—

Nothing in this world is without change. EXCEPT the fact that chance is inevitable. Change is both redesign and consistency, alteration and steadfastness, action and meditation. To be successful, let your approach constantly adapt to an ever changing world, but let your character be unwavering.

—

To change is one thing. To be transformed is to start anew.

—

To be a true friend is a much higher calling than to be a lover. To be both is ideal.

—

Death is nothing more than the period at the end of the sentence of your life.

—

Every number is an entity, and therefore a one of some type. In other words, life does not really consist of many different numbers. It consists really of many different types of ones preceded by and maintained by the zero.

—

An athlete with character will be a winner despite the outcome of the game. Character is more important than victory. Ask Joe Gilliam, Super Bowl Champ. He sold his championship ring for drugs. That ring did nothing for his addiction.

—

Zero is not "this' or "that". It has no opposite. It just simply IS. And because it exists, it makes this and that possible.

—

I once heard someone say that their mathematician dad once told him that there is more infinity between One and Zero than there is in between one and the rest of Infinity. That got me thinking.

Numbers are not merely quantities, but qualities represented as quantities. One is wholeness. Two is duality. Three is creation. Four is form. Etc. That being said, those essences can also be examined as fractions. 1, 2, 3, 4 can also be 1/1, 1/2, 1/3, 1/4. To understand the meaning or the essence of the succession of fractions is a journey back to zero rather than a trek to the outer edges of the circle of life. Life is circular, and to get farther from the center creates more centrifugal force, more pulling away from the center.

Now, try counting inward.

One is the most powerful creation of the Zero, because it makes all other whole numbers possible. The fraction is aware of that in that it always has One above any other number. 1/1, 1/2, 1/3, etc. When we count that way, we are on a journey to our center rather than a trip outward and away. Whole numbers are akin to people who place their individuality above their oneness. 2/1, 3/1, 4/1, etc. Fractions, likewise, are akin to humility.

To "count" effectively in Life, we must remember that the truest essence of any number is the zero that precedes it. One is not just 1. It is really 01. Two is 02. Three is 03. Whole numbers are also entities. 03 is also 3/1. 02 is 2/1, etc. The essence of the whole number is that we are all One. The essence of the fraction is that our Oneness is about our individuality. The essence of truth is that Zero is our truest reality, above and beyond our individuality, even before our Oneness.

Zero is the center of the number line, so try counting with fractions, and let the learning you acquire from the secession of numbers carry you back to your origin.

—

In jubilation and in sadness, never lose the ability to stay calm.

—

Treat your career as if it were a privilege. See your profession with the same passion and desire as you would if you were about to lose it.

—

Happiness is a choice before it is a fact, and so is anger.

—

Never judge anything or anyone by appearance in terms of importance. The anus is equally as important as the eyes.

—

Respect is like love minus the affection.

—

One is the number that unites all other numbers. One is like Zero on earth. Infinity is a giant One. Zero makes One possible.

—

My goal is not for this result or that result but to bring some character or quality to this circumstance or that circumstance.

—

Passion at its best deepens the experience of rationality. At its worst it is reckless.

—

Love wants to help someone be the best version of himself or herself.

—

Life is not just the things that happen to you. It is more about the context that you put them in.

—

The internet gives us many advantages. With that technology we can do many more things that were previously possible. In my opinion, it is fake freedom, because as we gain many advantages, we become more dependent. Dependence and freedom cannot co-exist. One who is dependent is not truly free.

—

All things that we see get their meaning from the unseen.

—

"I remember when phones were dumb, and people were smart."
  Gordy Knudtson

—

You don't have to change the world. Just make it better than it is right now.

—

Victory is short lived. What is much more important is who you become on the way to winning. Victory passes. Championships pass quickly, but character lives on.

—

Today is the only time this will happen.

—

Sin always exists in the past. The present is free of the past. Every moment is sparkling clean. As far as I am concerned, you are sinless right now.

—

The true mystery of life lies in nothingness and space, because matter itself is made of atoms, and there is much space within the building blocks of matter.

—

Taking full responsibility for a wrongdoing involves more than a sincere apology to the immediate victims of the transgression. It also includes a complete ownership of the action and a tangible signal of your intention to move forward in a way that shows that you have learned from your error in judgment to those you have wronged, including those who care for you...for you have wronged them too.

—

It is more important to see the beauty of the moment than perceive the secrets of the universe. The most important thing you can learn is that they are one and the same.

—

When you are the beneficiary of someone's benevolence, it is not enough to be grateful. You must also show your gratitude.

—

The depth of gratitude increases the potential for the height of joy.

—

Extremes are not as important as the lessons learned between them.

Patience is good in that it embodies the belief that all is well. It is a useful tool of the psyche, and like all tools there are times when it is not useful also. Wisdom is knowing when to use what tool. It is not wise to be patient in a fire.

—

No one gets to infinity by counting. True knowledge is not learned one lesson at a time. The Infinite cannot be reached one step at a time. What is infinite can be felt, experienced, lived, but it cannot be spoken, for words are finite. Counting, lessons, and steps are tools meant to be put down after their usefulness. Truth is realized by looking within the number or the lesson, not by continually going to the next one. Truth is realized or experienced, or even better, it is remembered. Remembering implies that we knew the Truth at one point before the journey. Even in the Bible, It does not say, "go out and seek" God. It says, "be still and know" God.

———

Achievements only have meaning in a finite existence. Degrees and steps are merely tools to help us to learn to put the tools down and experience. One cannot count to infinity. In fact, continually counting insures that you never get there.

———

A lesson is truly learned when you no longer have to think about it to put it into use.

———

If you believe that this life is an illusion, let me see you hold your imaginary breath, and let me know what happens. I'll wait...

———

Our finite identity, our finite selves, our finite lives of a few thousand days gives us our individuality. Our infinite life unites us all...for we are all sustained by the same zero.

———

Nutrition is as important as religion, maybe more.

———

The realization of your dreams doesn't start somewhere down the road. It starts today.

—

If you are a student, get into the habit of doing all of your homework, not so much because of what it teaches you, but do it to get in the habit of doing the hard work required. Work ethic is one of the most important factors on the road to success. Very few people on the road to success get a chance to pick and choose the work they will and won't do.

—

Always maintain a favorable healthy self image. If God Himself loves you, then who are you to feel differently?

—

Incorrect accusations without proof can be as damaging as wrongdoing with proof. Don't participate in either.

—

A true winner is shown as much by how he or she handles defeat as by whether or not he or she was the victor of the contest.

—

Inner peace is a greater gift than outer wealth.

—

The power of music and the arts is transformative, and the educational system must look to the arts and music, especially if it wants to change the trajectory of a failing school.

—

True love is transformative, and even the most evil person will change himself or herself for a chance to continue to feel it.

—

Hatred requires effort because the true nature of man is to love. Love, focus, and action transform culture. It requires very clear thinking and more than good intentions, for love can be a non-violent protest or the very active protection of innocent people. That is what makes it difficult, for the goals of love CAN contain violence. If you don't believe so, watch your own actions when your kids or loved ones are threatened. Love is transformative, but not all of its forms look like love on the surface.

—

Very few are anti-gun while dialing 911. Very few want smaller government when they are due their social security or in need of FEMA. Very few want less of "Big Brother" when terrorism hits them or their loved ones.

—

Heaven is my destination...but not yet...

—

The protection of the innocent is also a loving action, even when it contains violence. Martin Luther King had a chance, because the country was defended, and that defense involved some violence somewhere. I don't think Hitler could have been stopped by non-violence alone.

—

Nothing is more beautiful than the face of the one you love as you wake them from sleep with a kiss…ok, a few kisses…

—

The expertise of an individual too often is at the expense of the team…or the band.

—

Always be more concerned with character than talent. My parents, especially my mother, taught this to the point that even Rudy, in his mental illness, was the most loving person, even as he was really being done wrong by those around him, who should have been taking care of him. We get through the tough times with character, not talent…and tough times are inevitable.

—

Numbers make all things possible. The difference in all matter is determined by the number of electrons, protons, and neutrons in the atoms and the number and configuration of atoms in a molecule. Numeration defines and determines every facet of our lives, and zero makes every number possible. So in truth, numbers define our existence and give its parts differentiation, but Zero is what makes existence possible.

—

Bless this food to our use,
    And us to thy service.
Make us ever mindful
    For the needs of others.
        In Jesus' name,
            Amen

(That is how my mother taught us to bless the food before every meal. We would all say it together…asking God to bless the food and us also, keeping us vigilant for the needs of other people…a great gift of blessing from my Mom. I wonder who taught her that prayer?)

———

Bless this food
   That it help to
Keep our bodies strong,
   Our minds clear,
And our hearts pure.
   In Jesus' name,
      Amen

(This prayer came to me one day in the 80s. Now my kids and some of their friends say it too.)

———

Unseen does not mean non-existent.

———

Listening, not just speaking, is essential to communication.

———

Monetary wealth can create more problems than it solves and requires more character, not less, once it is attained.

———

To truly be free is more than just an opportunity to exist without rules. To truly be free, we must know the rules or laws that we are free from, otherwise we are destructive. To be free of illness requires that we know the laws of nutrition. To eat freely without that knowledge causes illness. To musically improvise freely requires knowledge of music theory, or the "free" playing collides with the music. True freedom is more like being in tune with natural order of things than it is anarchy. Freedom is more celebration than rebellion.

—

The older I get, I ask "why" less and accept things more.

—

Is the music industry a game? Music itself is not a game. One can even say music is sacred. But "industry" is the selling of a product in exchange for money, and like any industry it is indeed a game. Know the difference between the music and the industry. Honor the music, but learn the rules of the game.

Be a celebrity with integrity.

—

Why do I strive to excel? To set myself apart from my fellow man? No! I strive to be at my best, to excel, to show everyone that they can do it too…for inclusiveness.

—

If your life ended today, how would you feel about the life you have lived so far?

—

Those were the days. These are the days.

—

We as people tend to try to hold onto things too long. We love familiarity. When we have something good we want to stop there and relish in it forever. But time marches on, and nothing stays the same. You can only chew a perfect piece of fruit for so long. Your favorite song comes to an end. Friends move away. Loved ones pass on. So, what do we do then if nothing good will last?

Keep this in mind. That goodness DOES indeed endure…even past the moment or the person that gave it to you. I remember exactly what it felt like to embrace my mom's wisdom or my dad making me laugh. I can feel precisely how it felt to make the greatest music with all FIVE brothers. I can pass my mother's wisdom on because I was paying attention at the time. So, embrace the moments, or the friends, or the family, or the music, whatever it is, and internalize that goodness, knowing that its essence will always remain…even when the friends, family, moment, or song has long passed.

—

Life is indeed bittersweet because it ends in death, and within the bittersweetness of our own lives are a thousand smaller scenes of losing what we love.

—

Happiness is a combination of holding on and letting go.

—

Love does not always look like love. The protection of love is loving too, and sometimes that protection involves violence. Weapons and violence should ONLY be used as a last resort. Their purpose is to get us to a state where they are no longer necessary and love can prevail.

—

Having character makes the world better even if the rest of the world does not get a chance to see that it's better.

—

Gratitude is an essential component of happiness.

—

Nothing or zero is never meaningless, because "nothing" is always potential and everything that is something started from nothing. Everything that exists started with potential. What is potential except a zero with possibilities?

—

Enlightenment refers to gaining more understanding or awareness than you had before. It is useful to be enlightened…not so useful to think that you are ahead or behind anyone else. No matter how long you have been counting, you are no closer to infinity than the person that never started to count. The same thing goes for "enlightenment".

—

In a civilized well running society it is enough for adults to do their fair share…But when we have a problem with our young people, when too many of our youth are at risk, then doing our fair share is not enough. When our young people are astray, it requires that adults go above and beyond the call of duty.

Every "problem child" represents at least one adult who has let him or her down and therefore represents the need for at least one adult to step forward and exceed the adult's "fair share".

Let's do all that we can for this generation, because they are our only hope for the future.

—

Young people DO need to be responsible for their actions. But we, as parents and adults, need to be better examples and teachers. Kids pick on the same people that adults make fun of or disrespect…gays, fat people, Muslims, Mexicans, poor people, etc…

Where do you think they learned it from?

———

There is a joke that says, "How do you make a musician complain? You get him a gig."

Too often with success, we are still not satisfied with what we have strived so hard for. The "sixteen passenger van tour" is now on a tour bus. The few hundred dollars per week is now thousands of dollars per gig…plus per diem. Terrible hotels where you had to share a room are now Ritz Carlton's and Four Seasons in a room you don't have to share with anyone. Yet, we still complain. "This catering sucks!" or "Why didn't we fly instead of this long bus ride?"

As best you can, be grateful at all times, and remain vigilant not to become someone you would have hated when you were struggling.

———

No sustainable happiness exists without gratitude. Without gratitude there is always something else to complain about.

———

I have heard it said that "All we need is love." It is indeed a beautiful thing to say but oh so naive. Love is a powerful force, and like any force, it requires that we know the rules or that force can cause destruction.

Water, wind, electricity, etc. all require us to abide by strict rules for their force to be non-destructive. The same goes for love. Love needs understanding, because love without understanding is merely passion, and passion without direction is akin to an active firehose with no one to direct the stream. For that same hose to be helpful, it needs direction and guidance, like any force.

All we need is love? No, we equally need understanding.

—

The One contains all the essence of the Zero with the added ingredient of specificity. The One is the son of the Zero with all the attributes of its father except that its specificity gives it a start and a finish. One starts "here" and ends "there". One is the basis of all creation for as long as Creation exists.

—

If Nelson Mandela could keep his dignity while enduring the harshest of circumstances, caring for the condition of the hearts of his perpetrators in place of revenge...

If Ann Frank still believed in the goodness of all people while being hunted like an animal...

If Martin Luther King could transform a nation with non-violence, faith, and understanding, while enduring violence, ungodliness, and brutal lack of care for one's fellow man based only on skin color...

Then I am inspired to be at my best at all times through all things.

—

Weak is the one whose character is swayed by circumstance.

—

James Brown, Sly Stone, Mandrill, Parliament Funkadelic, The Ohio Players, etc. is what I call "big afro funk". New Jack Swing is what I call "curl activator funk". Do NOT spray curl activator in my perfectly good afro!

—

Never complain wholeheartedly. Always leave a portion of your consciousness to examine the validity and context of your grievance.

—

Nothing takes away the transformative power of artistry faster than arrogance.

—

One who finds the beauty in oneself is much more likely to find someone to share it with.

—

A birthday is a death day eventually, but do not let the sorrow of the latter overshadow the joy of the former.

—

We know that we think, and therefore we think that we know. Too often, we are wrong on both accounts.

—

True friendship is the highest form of love. In fact, if lovers are not also friends, their love is unstable. Friendship that is true remains steady as infatuation, affection, and romance ebb and flow.

—

As human beings, we are a living set of conditions, a certain height and weight with a specific personality that is influenced largely by our environment. We will live a specific number of days in specific locations around specific people in specific circumstances. Where unconditional love is highly improbable, unconditional friendship is available and preferred, for true friendships last where love affairs end.

—

Friendship is the seed of true love. Where love desires the company of another, seeks its affection, and wants love in return, true friendship only desires what is best for the other, even if what is best does not include him or her.

—

The hardest thing in life is to live up to your own expectations.

—

In our attempt to be the best that we can be, it is important to do the best that we can do. And in viewing what we have done, it is important to look at ourselves in terms of the quality of our actions, more than it is to judge our actions by their distance to perfection.

—

Perfection is an aspiration more than it is a requirement.

—

Is it coincidence that "lawyer" and "liar" sound so much alike? You can hardly say one without saying the other, and too often they are interchangeable.

—

I have said before that "Being onstage is a performance. A beautiful lie. A fabrication for the right reason." Let me elaborate...
The stage elevates the performer and puts him or her literally and figuratively in his or her best light. It physically forces the audience to

look up to the artist when the truth of the matter is that the performer is no more or less than the viewing audience.

A performer is not the truth. A person on the witness stand cannot "perform" because a performance is not the whole truth. The inhabitants of the stage are there for an exhibition, a rendition of the truth for the purpose of art and "inner attainment" or entertainment. True artistic rendition is indeed a beautiful fabrication of reality onstage for the right reasons. This "beautiful lie" unites the performer and the audience, and at its best elevates all involved. The actor, the musician, and the artist in reality are no more or less than the attending audience. Yet, for a time, the artist and audience agree on these artificial parameters for the sake of art and entertainment.

The stage, in a way, is a fabricated set of circumstances containing real people, performing or acting, for the purpose of truth…a beautiful lie for the right reason of true art and all of its benefits.

———

We are all different, yet we are all the same, carrying around the different names, inside telling the story of the One.

———

We all helped create this mess
    Christian, Muslim, Atheist
Help us all to come together
    We can't love You
Until we love each other

———

One of the downsides of politics is that it too often causes people to choose sides before they know the issues.

———

This life starts with birth and ends in death, and within this life of ours are countless episodes of losing the things that we love and the people that we adore. Always appreciate your blessings, for at some point all of them will be gone.

———

It is easy to fall in love. It is harder to stay in love.

———

To have someone who believes in you wholeheartedly, to have someone who is always happy to hear from you, to have someone who you know beyond the shadow of a doubt will always be there for you, no matter what, in any circumstance…is indeed priceless.

———

Blessed beyond measure is the life with the opportunity to be artistic and have that art appreciated.

———

A humble person who has not realized his talent has a chance at greatness. A talented person who has not realized his humility has no chance of true greatness. Humility is the foundation and the seed of true greatness, for when humility is lost, "greatness" always descends into arrogance.

———

Sign every autograph and take every picture if at all possible.

———

Always be at your best, and when you fall short, always be self forgiving. Being self forgiving is essential for those of us who are imperfect.

—

Forgiveness is not only for other people.

—

At all times as best you can, keep in your conscious mind reasons to be grateful. Gratefulness will shine light on your darkest days. Like fireflies in the night, gratitude can beautify the darkness.

—

The chance to see the world because I can sing and play…I am not exactly sure why…but I promise to try and make the best of it.

—

Always remember that there are a countless number of things that happen in your favor even for you to have a "bad" day.

—

Gratitude! Humility!

—

Not all music is made on an instrument.

—

Music is audible order and tangible harmony; audible harmony and tangible order.

—

The heart keeps the head from being cynical and dispassionate. The head keeps the heart from being unrealistic and impractical. Wisdom is not just a balance of the two, but in my opinion, wisdom is knowing what proportion of which to apply to any given situation.

—

My brothers and I never argue. We grew up not arguing. My mother would not allow us to do so, and even though it helped us to get along with each other, I cannot say with 100% certainty that we came out ahead of the families who did argue but worked through their differences.

—

The One determines how you are. The Zero determines that you are.

—

Everyone can be viewed as crazy from someone's point of view.

—

Too often, anger is a feeble attempt to offset one's feeling of powerlessness.

—

Philosophy, at its best, gives us insight into the nuances of life, truth, and the nature of things. At is worst, philosophy attempts to obscure the obvious.

—

One gives us our individuality. Zero gives us our existence.

—

Is there anything more potentially dangerous than a passionate group of people who are uninformed or misinformed and still very opinionated?

—

No love affair will last that is not founded in friendship and respect for one another.

—

Your time on Earth won't be long. So do your dance and sing your song.

—

Criticism of one's self is sometimes appropriate for the ones who strive to be at their best, but it should never exist alone. Self forgiveness should always hold the hand of self criticism.

—

Inner peace is a greater gift than outer wealth and is necessary if outer wealth is to bring any lasting happiness.

—

My mother used to say that saying what you will "never" do is your first stop to doing it.

—

When deciding whether the glass is half full or half empty, keep in mind that the glass itself is both a privilege and a blessing.

—

A true leader is ultimately judged by results and not by characteristics. A person who has the qualities to lead or be in charge but does not act cannot be considered a good leader. A good leader must not only execute but must show by example how others may do so.

—

Do not be so eager to be a donor of criticism if you have trouble being a recipient.

—

We get through the tough times with character, not talent…and tough times are inevitable.

—

The past can be looked at like a rear-view mirror on an automobile. It can give you useful information, but if you look at it too long, you lose sight of where you are going. The only way you can look at a rear-view mirror consistently without crashing is by not moving forward. The same goes for looking at the past.

—

Science reality is better than science fiction.

—

Like water, one who does not move forward becomes stagnant.

—

Love can be expressed with specifics, but its essence is non specific. Specificity is "here" and not "there". Love, which is everywhere, is not bound by a situation or dynamic. A specific can express love, but the love it expresses is beyond the confines of finite existence.

—

Being on time requires no talent but is an integral necessity of the talented.

—

Ask yourself this. If you do not have the basic discipline to be consistently on time, do you deserve to be successful?

—

What you think of me is not my concern. The distance between what I think of me and what I am makes all the difference.

—

Most of life, maybe all of it, is musical, but living it is much more improvisation than it is reading music.

—

Any decision made with testosterone need a second opinion.

—

A large part of character is maintaining your integrity when you don't have to.

—

I once was complaining of long days of driving my girlfriend to work, hours in the studio, picking her up from work, and then gigging that night. My Aunt Anne Lois said, "Well, it ain't picking cotton."

I have never forgotten that.

—

What is religion without a life well lived attached to it? A well lived life without religion is worth much more than religion without character, discipline, and self control.

—

Determination is just patience with intensity.

—

Self importance would always hold the hand of humility.

—

It is just as important to see the worth of others as it is to see your own.

—

Arrogance is the over reaction of a person who secretly fears his or her own lack of self worth or importance. Haughtiness is over compensation.

—

Being yourself is the most unavoidable thing in life…yet, the hardest thing to do.

—

It is not the responsibility of the audience to like you.

—

Gratitude is a necessity for anyone who wants true happiness.

—

In one sense, we don't owe each other anything. In another sense, we owe each other everything. We owe each other respect and at least a desire not to harm one another. In a sense, that's nothing. In another, it is everything.

—

One of the reasons that James Brown was so successful is that he was a pure version of himself. He was very real, and the fact that he was such a great example was magnified by the fact that he was so accessible to the people who admired him. Every person fortunate enough to gain any measure of fame and fortune could, and in my opinion should, use James Brown as an example.

—

The mystery of numbers has less to do with their quantity and more to do with why those quantities stay together.

—

A society that is divided and misinformed or uninformed is ripe for manipulation and exploitation by its leaders.

—

Your track record enters the room when you do and is reinforced by consistency. It speaks for itself and does not need for you to do so.

—

Zero is essence of life, and One is the fabric of life.

—

Light and darkness cannot co-exist. Darkness in the presence of light ceases to exist. Darkness can only thrive where there is a blocking of the light to create shadow. Light is indeed eternal, but blockages are not. Evil senses that its days are numbered, and that is why it always acts out. Evil is demonstrative in an attempt to show you its superiority over Love. Darkness' "grand finale", its "exhibit A" of its power, is death and the fear it generates. But death is a part of life, like a period at the end of a great sentence. Do not live in fear of death or evil. To love requires no effort. To hate, resent, fight, and hide from light is tiring over time. In the small picture, evil is terrifying. In the larger picture…eventually…Evil, no matter how bad it acted…Hitler, Mussolini, Jim Crow Laws, Apartheid…all of them wind up working for the light as an example of what NOT to do and how NOT to be.

—

Death is nothing more than the period at the end of the sentence of your great life here on this Earth.

—

A person or society that feels that justice is not possible has no incentive to be peaceful. Peace is a by-product of justice, and where there is injustice, there is no lasting peace.

—

Specifics never tell the whole story, for life is always more than the sum of its parts.

—

Try to never shut off your excellence.

—

What good is forgiveness if it only applies to a few people?

—

Desire needs more than passion. It needs a plan.

—

Take me to the water before the well runs dry
    Let me see the light before I close my eyes
Use my inner vision so that I can see
    I'm a man on a mission, a warrior at peace

Help me to be righteous while I break the rules
    Let me lose my temper while I keep my cool
Live no fabrication so I can just be me
    Thrive on liberation so I can still be free

Let me be a leader, leading from behind
    Help me keep my focus while I expand my mind
Always stand up when I fall but never break my neck
    Always speak what's on my mind but never disrespect

Help me push the limits while I stay in bounds
    With my head up in the clouds, my feet on the ground
Let me see the future but respect the past
    Help me hit like Rock & Roll, be smooth like Jazz

Help me fight for justice while I keep the peace
   Help me stand up on my feet, praying on my knees
Help me make the money but still share the wealth
   Let me be the people's champ keeping to myself

Take me to the water before the well runs dry
   Let me see the light before I close my eyes
Use my inner vision so that I can see
   I'm a man on a mission, a warrior at peace

—

One who disrespects another does so unbeknownst that he really disrespects himself more.

—

Sometimes you have to see people in their best light because they can't do it.

—

I saw a guy with a tee shirt that had written on it, "Sarcasm is the body's natural defense against stupidity." So I looked at him and said, "Yeah, right!"

—

No adult can teach a child effectively without first being a good example.

—

The older I get, the more I remember my mother mentioning the importance of having "a strong foundation" in life.

—

Mistakes are only mistakes in the small picture. In the big picture everything happens for a reason.

—

Not every change comes by fighting. The river changes the land by calm consistency. Light removes darkness simply by being itself. Fighting should be your last resort, not your first.

—

Is there any joy greater than the joy of connecting a young person with his or her potential?

—

Strive to see beauty in everyone.

—

Forgiveness operates from the premise that we are, in the truest sense, part of the same One. Therefore to deny forgiveness to anyone is to deny forgiveness to ourselves.

—

Do your best never to let your passion and opinion of the facts make you insensitive.

—

I met a woman who told me of her late father who had a genius mind but was an atheist, agnostic at best. He would ask her, "How can you believe in God? How can you have faith in something you cannot see?" They had many long discussions on the subject. One

day in the discussion she said, "Do you know I love you?" He said, "Of course I do!" She said, "But how can you prove it?" He paused and said....
"Now, I get it!"

———

When punishing a child in any manner, it is imperative that they know they are wrong, otherwise you reinforce in their mind the idea of injustice.

———

Dropping all the bombs by the plane and the jet
   Holding hostages 'til conditions are met
They're angry at the west, we're lighting up the east
   And all the killing done in the name of peace

———

I have heard it said that fighting for peace is like having sex for contraception. Although it is very humorous, in my opinion, it is only partly true.
Fighting for peace is more akin to the controlled burning of a skilled firefighter that strategically torches part of the forest to contain and ultimately eliminate the raging wildfire. As with all fighting, it should be done as a last resort.

———

Do not be afraid of mistakes. A person who has more maturity has gained his or her added wisdom by experience. How does one get more experience? By making mistakes.

———

In the music business as in any business, you adapt or risk becoming irrelevant.

—

Chances are, your child, once he or she learns to speak, speaks with your dialect and your speech patterns. They learned it very well, not by any particular thing you said or told them. Your young ones are constantly watching, learning, and becoming some version of you, so be a good example as best you can.

—

Whether or not you believe in God, religion, or meditation, trust the value of silence.

—

Life on this Earth is a constant now that is always changing and a constant changing that is always now.

—

Experience can help you to acquire knowledge, but of the two, experience is greater.

—

There is a time for meditation. There is a time for action. Wisdom and clarity help us to determine which course of action or inaction to take.

—

I don't try to be at my best to make anyone else do anything in particular. I try to be at my best because I know it matters.

———

I matter. You matter.

———

In the words of my mother, who would always say this to us before we left, "Act like you ought to."

———

The fireman has no time for meditation when the house is burning. No one does. Meditation is valuable and important…but not at all times.

———

A young person who lives in poverty where violence is the norm, where crime is prevalent, who is sometimes undernourished, who lives where murder is common, that young person is in survival mode and probably does not have school or education as a priority. What is going wrong in the school (or right for that matter) is the end result of what is going wrong or right in their society, and to try to change one without changing the other is unrealistic, in my opinion.

———

It is important to dream. It is meaningless ONLY to dream. A dream can be the beginning step of a great endeavor or merely a symptom of the fact that you are asleep.

———

The infinite can be experienced. It cannot be grasped.

———

Not everyone that you would like to help wants your help.

—

It is good to be a leader, but even a leader needs guidance.

—

To enjoy the fullness of life, we must learn to let go, to not always be "in control". Life is immense with an unlimited amount of parameters and factors, too many to control. The constant attempt to check, test, and verify for the sake of the certainty and the absence of doubt is endless and eventually tiring. Learn to let go. Life understands you much better than you understand it, and it knows what you need more than you do.

—

We hold a grudge. We harbor resentment. We flash our temper and exact our wrath all in an attempt to make someone be who we wish them to be…in a feeble attempt to feel powerful. Yet, love is much more powerful, nourishing, and requires no effort for you to tear down your own walls.

—

The easiest and the hardest thing to do is just be yourself.

—

"Who are you?" is the most important question in life, and the absence of that answer becomes an obstacle when it is time to just be yourself. Why should it be that that which is unavoidable, being yourself, is difficult to do? Know who you are, and life begins to make much more sense. Without that knowledge, life remains a mystery, and your decisions remain a gamble.

———

You don't play music or sports with just your talent. You also play with your character. Character without talent is acceptable. Talent without character is always disappointing at some point.

———

I heard someone famous comment that to be successful, one must take a "leap of faith" and jump off of the "cliff of life". My response:

My mother would say, "You are successful already. Other people just don't know it yet." I say, whether you jump or not, have character. Have things in perspective. Be honest. Love people. Love yourself. Be grateful. And whether or not you jump, your life will be fulfilled.

Many jump. Many have parachutes that open but have no character. Life is not so much about soaring as it is about having your feet on the ground. Not every one is a jumper. But the immensity of life is there for those who choose to stay on the ground, too. You see, the truth is not OUT there, the truth is IN you.

Jump if you want. Stay on the ground if you choose. But know the truth. You don't have to jump to hug your momma and tell her you love her.

———

When change occurs, the easiest thing to do is to do nothing. The hardest thing to do is to accept that you've done nothing. The result, too often, is to complain about the way things used to be while doing nothing.

———

Never let your concentration be at the expense of what's going on around you.

———

116

Faith in general is good, but faith needs to be vetted by some other qualities or it is likely to lead us astray. It is imperative for faith to have vision or it can easily lead to disappointment or even danger. Remember, they ALL had faith in Jim Jones before they drank the Kool-Aid.

—

It is more important to know who you are on your journey than it is to know where you are going.

—

Wishes and desires both want the same things. They both dream of the same goals. The difference is that desire embraces the process to reach the goal, and wishes never get past merely dreaming because of the perceived difficulty of the process ahead.

—

Do not let your ideas of what you think that future will hold overshadow your appreciation of the present.

—

That which is infinite needs no defense, for the infinite has no foe. Our spirit is not bound by time or space. Our bodies however will not be here forever. Your body is a temporary vehicle of your infinite spirit that enables you to test out your belief systems.

—

It is noble to be at your best when things are at their worst, better to be at your best at all times.

—

Entertainment at its worst is merely a spectacle. At its best, entertainment facilitates inner attainment and is beneficial for both the audience and the artist.

———

When there is nothing you can do, it is best to do nothing calmly.

———

I have never been bothered by the crying of a baby. They feel sadness and misery just like adults, but they cannot verbalize their sorrow and pain. The baby has no other choice. The adult, however, too often, chooses his or her wailing or complaining when tolerance or patience was an option.

———

It is important to know the difference between an inconvenience and a problem.

———

The patient person must be vigilant for complacency and procrastination like the decisive person must be wary of impulsiveness and impatience.

———

It is not enough merely to have faith.
    It matters what you have faith in.
It is not enough just to believe.
    It matters what you believe in.
It is not enough merely to be an example.
    It matters what you are an example of.

Being in love happens so effortlessly that it is easy to forget that it carries with it enormous responsibility.

—

Forgiveness must be complete or your lack of forgiveness will forever remain a spark or an ember capable of reigniting the issue that you wish would remain in the past.

—

Your life is the only life shortened or made miserable by the underlying resentment of incomplete forgiveness. Forgiveness is as much for YOUR benefit as the one that you think is wrong...maybe more.

—

Love is the strongest of all emotions and requires no effort. You must hold on to hatred and cling to resentment for those emotions to manifest. Love is opposite.

To love, you let go.

—

Remember, even a bad day is a privilege.

—

I am not sure how much a school teacher is paid...but it is NOT enough!!!

—

Joy is gratitude's view of Life, and laughter is a situational expression of joy in spite of all of life's shortcomings and peculiarities.

—

It is important to find your way when things don't go your way.

—

The ideas and precepts of forgiveness are often much more acceptable until someone does you wrong.

—

You cannot raise a child "by the book". Every child is unique. It takes the instincts of a parent to know what is best for his or her child, and it takes the guts to follow it through, especially when the child wholeheartedly disagrees.

—

When you don't know what to do next, do whatever you do at this moment with quality.

—

Can happiness be complete where forgiveness is incomplete? To forgive incompletely is similar to carrying in the trunk of your car the boulder that flattened your tire.

—

Never lose the ability to see someone in a favorable light, even if that person doesn't see himself, herself, or you the same way.

—

Happiness is a decision before it is a fact. Make a decision to be happy, but do not lie to yourself if you are not.

—

Lead singing, a large portion of it, is done most successfully by having lots of confidence and a sense of delivery. A confident lead singer with imperfect pitch has a better chance of success than an unconfident singer with perfect pitch, especially if there is a stage involved.

—

Zero is beauty, and all of its numbers show you how it is beautiful.

—

If you found out that you only had a few days to live, how would you feel about the life you are living?

—

The old Crusades or the new jihad. There's too much killing in the name of God.

—

Zero is nothing, but it is the reason everything has existence.

—

Be a leader when the time is right, when you are the most qualified, or when others want you to lead them. Never attempt to be a leader just for the sake of being in charge or above others. There is no shame in being a follower if someone knows where you are going and you don't.

A true leader leads much more by example than by giving orders, and those that follow do so willingly knowing that leader has their best interest at heart.

—

When you don't eat you realize that the day is long. Twenty-four hours is PLENTY of time!

—

The highest calling of music is inspiration. The highest calling of inspiration is transformation. Art at its best is both.

—

Love is the emotion of life
Beauty is the complexion of love
Life is the canvas of All
Truth is the common denominator

—

It takes some character to find a way to think positively of someone you feel has wronged you and not judge him or her solely by his or her indiscretion.

—

He or she who cannot forgive burns the same bridge that he or she will one day need to cross.

—

Strive to never let your heart harden. The mighty oak is destroyed by the same storm that the blade of grass survives.

—

Never judge a person's whole life by any one action in the same manner that you would not want anyone to form an opinion or make their decisions about you based on a time when you were not at your best.

—

We always have money when its time to start a war...never got a dime when it's time to feed the poor.

—

People are not perfect, but they do contain perfection. No two people are alike. That in itself is a type of perfection. If everything happens for a reason, then even our mistakes are part of a greater perfect plan.

—

We don't have full access to the big picture. All we can do is do our best in the little one.

—

Doting over a woman is not the same as caring for her. It is important to know the difference.

—

Most of the greatest people I have met are people few have heard of. Do not confuse fame for greatness.

The finite is a temporary vessel for the infinite, and the two give birth to creation.

—

It is important to know the difference between having an opinion and taking a stance.

—

A perfect circle is a shape that exists because there is a center that makes all points of the circle possible. You can't see the center, but the quality of the circle proves its existence. The same goes for the Circle of Life. That living circle is proof that there is a living center that makes all aspects of the Circle of Life possible.

—

Success is gained by a combination of opportunity and will power. One is a gift and one is choice, and it is important to be aware enough to recognize the gifts of opportunity so that you choose where and how to use your will power wisely.

—

It is as important to recognize the value of others as it is to have self importance. In fact, your self importance is out of balance unless and until you recognize the value of others.

—

I have heard it said that, "All you need is love." I understand the premise, but in my opinion, you equally need understanding. In this world it is also important to understand the context and ramifications of that love.

Love is powerful, and we all love something. But love of family can cause fights with other families who love theirs just as passionately. Love of another's spouse, no matter how sincere the love, is problematic. Love of Country sometimes fuels war. Love without understanding is too often passion without control, and uncontrolled passion is or can be dangerous and/or destructive.

—

The heart feels what the head doesn't, and the head sees what the heart doesn't see, and somehow we are supposed to make sense of it all.

—

Intuition, as strong as it may be, is evidence and not fact. It is wise to give intuition time to reveal its validity or illegitimacy. Nothing stings like accusations based on intuitions and feelings that were later undone by the facts.

—

Every gain is eventual loss. Every life is eventual death, for nothing on this earth lasts forever.

—

The best way to make yourself feel better is to help someone else to feel better.

—

One who gives freely to others but has trouble accepting the benevolence of others is in danger of engaging in an easily disguised silent arrogance that says, "I am more worthy of giving than you are."

—

For one's distaste of racism to be fully true and pure, it must exist under the larger umbrella of man's inhumanity to man. Who can truly hate racism of any kind that accepts sexism, gender bias, or discrimination based on sexual orientation? Our disdain for discrimination ought not be partial.

——

Live never to look down on anyone. Do your best to not be judgmental. You don't know a person's story or what it was that got them to do the thing you disapprove of.

——

Remind yourself that you are not the epicenter of normal nor the poster child of how we all should be. Everyone is different.

To see is unthinkable for the blind. To stand would be a miracle for the wheel chair bound. To feel a touch is impossible for the paralyzed. To sleep in a warm bed or to be looked upon with respect is extremely difficult for the homeless. Enjoy the life that you have, and from time to time take a look at it from the perspective of those less fortunate.

——

As great as you are, you are not special. Or, if you are special, you are no more special than anybody else.

——

I matter. You matter. You and I matter.

——

I am not seeking perfection, but I am constantly seeking improvement.

—

Life has a way of using imperfection…perfectly.

—

Today will never happen again so make the best of it.

—

An important part of fixing a problem is not over reacting to it. Over reacting to a situation too often causes the other side of the dynamic to either dig in their heels or over react themselves.

—

Do your best to appreciate what you have in a larger capacity than you wish for what you don't have.

—

To think a thought, one merely must be awake, but to think the thought, examine the idea, and be conscious of its potential impact and ramifications, one must be aware.

—

Know where you stand at all times. Take a stand only when necessary.

—

We are not on this Earth to be to be perfect, but we are here to be genuine.

—

I am not sure why my life is full, joyful, and gives me the privilege of travel to many exciting locations while others toil and struggle in poverty, in war torn areas or areas where opportunities are few. I cannot answer that. But I can and do pledge to do my best to be at my best, not just for my own gain but also for those who don't have my opportunity. I strive to be "ever mindful for the needs of others" like we used to say as children before every meal.

—

Health is more important than health care. Healthy food is more expensive than unhealthy food but less expensive than being ill.

—

In turbulent situations strive to be one who is calm. Keep in mind that even the worst hurricane has a very calm center, a very peaceful center where birds fly and the sun shines. And it is the peaceful eye of the hurricane that determines the storms direction and power.

—

Zero is nothing, yet it is everywhere.

—

What is time but zero that we get a chance to use and handle? What is space but zero that we get a chance to play in? Without time and space, life would be a pile of beautiful creations without any time to get nowhere.

—

128

Not all police officers are bad, but if the same percentage of car seats, strollers, or air bags killed people we would recall them.

—

Nothing is nowhere.
    Everything is everywhere.
        Nothing is everywhere.
            Everywhere is nothing.

—

Advice for a young couple or any couple...NEVER let your relationship get to a place where your mate feels that someone else understands them better than you do.

—

Where justice seems not possible, peace is not probable.

—

There is no harm done in people telling you what you cannot do. All the damage is done when you accept it.

—

To be in love is beautiful and intoxicating, like a dream. To stay in love and be in a relationship is still beautiful, but the relationship requires you to be much more sober.

—

Like sports, life is a game. Unlike sports the purpose of the game of life has less to do with the final score and more to do with who you become during the game despite the final outcome.

—

If you are fortunate enough to be loved by many, do your best to handle it with care. Do your best to let them know that you love them back. Do your best to keep them from thinking that you are something that they are not. Do your best to create a sense of connection if at all possible.

—

For some, it is enough to tell them that they matter. For others, they need more than words.

—

It is more important to work on your capacity for greatness than it is to work on your path to greatness. If one is great, much of the path will take care of itself. Greatness needs a plan, but it also needs clarity to see the additional opportunities that were never planned for.

—

If you find it hard to say you are sorry, show with your actions that you are a different person than the one who caused the indiscretion.

—

In life it is important to hold people accountable for their actions, and if at all possible, it is equally important to give them the chance to be better. Do not let the actions of others give you a reason to harden your heart.

—

My mother believed in the power of praising a child. She knew that a young person that did right and received loving acknowledgment of their actions would be self motivated to do it again. She used to tell me, "You have the patience of Job." I had no idea who "Job" was, but if she said it was good, that was enough for me.

I am patient by nature, but because my mother identified part of my goodness by praising me it motivated me to be even more patient. She let me know, not just that I was good, but by her praise and acknowledgment, she let me know how I was good, and that is good parenting.

—

Greatness is not something that is determined only by your accomplishments. The person who gives their time to the elderly despite a busy schedule, or the teacher that goes above and beyond for the benefit of the student, or the soldier who puts his or her safety on the line so that you don't have to...these people have the highest form of greatness. Higher is the level of greatness and character when it is exemplified in the absence of applause or in anonymity.

—

My mother knew that there was a good chance that her children would be famous, but fame was not her concern. She made sure we had principles to live by, morals, character, and what she called "a good foundation". She knew that if we had that solid foundation, our fame would be a good thing. She always wanted us to be good examples whether we were famous or not.

—

If your body is a temple, do your best to not let any garbage enter. A temple is meant to be sacred. Treat it as such.

—

Falling short of a desired goal is not the same as failure. If one learns from the experience of not reaching what was strived for, then what some call failure is, in truth, the seed of success. In my opinion, true failure can only exist where quitting is involved. A quitter is seldom successful.

——

I had a young musician ask me to help him "get to the next level" as an artist. I told him to start by doing everything he can at the level where he is.

——

Yes, Stevie Wonder is blind, but without the use of his eyes, he has more vision than most.

——

We don't need to strive to be a "color blind" society, but we should aspire to be a society where color is not an issue. Colors are too beautiful to ignore.

——

I just read that speaking is expressing what you already know, but listening gives you a chance to learn something new. No truer words were ever spoken.

——

In life, it is as important to accept forgiveness as it is to forgive. Do your best to never be a stumbling block on someone's road to redemption.

——

In the small picture, your narrative may seem to be written by what people say. Ultimately, your story will be written more by who you are than the opinions of others. Live less to have favorable headlines and more to have substance and character.

—

All things that we look to achieve in the big picture are available in the small picture.

—

Advice for anyone wanting a career in the music business…

My advice is to strive for more than fame. Start with being a person of substance. The strive for fame is an empty one. Even if you achieve it, you find that fame is empty UNLESS you have substance. We are, in a way, crazy for insisting to pursue what we KNOW is a long shot. Yet, we cannot be deterred or turned away. So, if we do not reach our goals, we have no one to blame. We chose this life. BUT, if our goal is to be substantive or meaningful, then whether or not we reach our goal of fame or notoriety we will be successful. The meaning that we seek from the big picture that we hope for is available right here in the small picture that we have today. Without character, without self respect, without respect for others, without substance, reaching our goal will still be empty. Again, I hear the words of my mother, Dorothy, and they ring truer everyday…

"We have enough good musicians…we need more good people!"

—

Where there is division, the question, "Who is right?" or "Who is wrong?" is less important than the question, "How do we move forward from here?"

—

The essence of life is expressed in its details but does not reside there. Details are specifics that show the precise beauty of the non specific. A kiss may express love, but love is beyond the kiss. Notes may give us a beautiful song, but the music is beyond the notes. Enjoy the details, but do not dwell on them. Instead, let them lead you to the essence. One cannot grasp the essence of life one detail at a time. It is tiring and impossible, for the parts are infinite. To experience the essence of life though, requires no effort, just a shift of attention, not on the details but between them. The immensity of life cannot be grasped, but it can be experienced.

—

Success in the music business has more to do with the quality of your connections than it does with the number of your connections. If you are fortunate enough to play music for a living, do your best to connect with your audience, and then nurture those connections. A musician whose goal is to form a bond with his or her audience plays music for the right reason.

—

Zero or nothingness is the essence of Life. Oneness is the theme or the goal of everything. No one can get to his or her essence, his or her truth without Oneness. One or Oneness is the way, the truth, and the life.

—

Jesus was known also known as "The One". Makes sense, right?

—

No one can effectively disrespect you if you maintain respect for yourself.

—

Our eyes help us to learn and discern, to see differences and interpret the world of finite separateness. When we want to feel what is and what has always been, when we want to experience meaning and essence, we close our eyes. Open eyes give us sight. Closed eyes can give us vision.

—

Rhythm is orderly repetition, and its purpose is to focus energy. That is true whether it be the frequency (the number of times something is repeated per second) of a sound wave, the beats per minute of a drum pattern, or your child's voice saying, "Dad, Dad, Dad, Dad, Dad, Dad…"

—

It is important to understand the value of focus. Focus is a vital part of life and an imperative factor of anyone's journey to success. But it matters what you focus on. Well placed focus can turn potential into reality. Misplaced focus is texting while driving and is the criminal's tool for picking your pocket.

—

Replace, if at all possible, your fear of death with an appreciation for all that life has to offer.

—

Nothing or no thing is not the same as non-existence. Life itself is not a "thing". It is what I call "meaningful existence". Meaning, like life, is broad and non-specific. Things are very specific and exist temporarily to focus life's aspects. In essence, "things" exist to show us precisely what "nothing" is.

—

Happiness that does not have gratitude and acceptance as its base exists on shaky ground.

—

Love everyone, if at all possible, but at all times do what you must.

—

Greater is the entertainer who recognizes that he or she is no better or more important than the audience.

—

If you put confetti in the wind it will show you the beauty of the breeze, and long after the journey of the beautiful paper is over, the wind still is as alive as ever. People are the beautiful confetti in the breeze of life.

—

Zero is peaceful because there is nothing, not a thing, to cause conflict.

—

Zero is peaceful because it has no parts to conflict. Zero is everywhere, and for that reason, peace is always possible.

—

A person need not ever hear the words God or Jesus spoken to live a principled, focused, and spiritual life. The essence of life lives in what you do with it, not what you call it.

—

Be careful of the use of the word "crazy". Everyone is crazy from someone's point of view.

—

To be and to do co-exist to one another like zero to one.

—

Zero "is", and One "does".

—

One is the body of zero, and like all finite numbers and things, it will return to zero when its job is done and its unique life is over.

—

Laughter is proof that joy is, at least for the time being, undeniable and irrepressible.

—

Evil is never eternal because evil always involves conflict, and conflict always involves at least two. Two is finite. Two is never eternal.

—

Do your best to always be at your best. Pay attention to the details and do your best to excel at them. Treat people as nicely as possible. Take you health seriously. Be mindful of what you say and do…and when you fall short, be quick to forgive yourself.

—

Try to see the goodness in others, even when they do their best to show you their worst.

———

Identifying someone by his or her worst attributes does not make you a better person, even when your findings seem to be accurate.

———

The largest ingredient in the recipe of success is work ethic.

———

Do not attend every party of anger and disrespect that you are invited to.

———

The quality of a circle is dependent upon the condition and stability of its center. You are the center of your circle of events.

———

In life, there is right and there is wrong, and then there is what is best.

———

I doubt social media is going away. Too many who complain about the effects of Facebook do so on Facebook.

———

The optimist is no closer to perfection than the pessimist, but he or she is a lot closer to his or her joy and happiness.

—

Eat as though your life depends on it. Eat as if eating is a high privilege. It always is.

—

Even helpful advice is badgering if the other person doesn't want to hear it.

—

I do want a President who is spiritual, but I don't want a President who takes the Country into war or makes decisions affecting millions because God told him or her to do it.

—

Money is neutral. It is neither bad nor good, but indeed it is a powerful magnifier of our goodness and virtue or our greed and inadequacy of character.

—

When two people are no longer in love, no longer on the same page, and the company of the other no longer brings joy, then the most loving thing that can be done is to move on. Move on honorably and respectfully, as painful as it may be to do so, in honor of the love and relationship that once was, for love and relationship, past or present, should always be respected.

—

Too often, we think of opposites as contradictory, contrary, and antagonistic. Those who oppose us or contradict us cause us stress. (Why don't they think like us or see the obvious truth?) Remember that opposites are the essential components of balance and create a truth larger than either opposing force or opinion.

—

What I think of me is much more important that what you think of me.

—

I was just given some grapes from a very nice older woman in the Cincinnati airport, and it dawned on me as she offered to share her healthy snack. Few things warm your heart more than the kindness of strangers.

—

Perception is everything. The statue of Venus is no more naked than a stripper or pin up girl. The statue of David is less naked than a Chippendale performer. One person's art is another's pornography.

—

If love is the essence of life, creativity is its expression and expansion.

—

It takes courage to step into your destiny. Be brave!

—

Life is less of what happens to you than it is the context you put those events into.

—

Love is a meaningful zero. It's not a thing, but it's everything.

—

I am not in control of what happens to me, but I am in control of who I am while it is happening to me.

—

A woman cannot be separated from her uterus, and therefore when she becomes pregnant it is her choice of whether or not she carries the pregnancy to term. We can argue the morality and even the legality of that choice, but we cannot separate the woman from that choice without becoming immoral.

—

It is important to know who you are and equally as important to understand how who you are fits with others. In music and in life, it is imperative to know who you are and likewise important to know your audience and bandmates.

—

A person who lives primarily in the basement has knowledge of that basement, knowledge backed by experience, but his or her thoughts on the rest of the house, at best, are opinion because he or she has never been or has limited experience in the other rooms or outside of the house.

Humans are living points of view, and like the person in the basement or any other part of the house, our views on the world, as impassioned as the may be, as correct or incorrect as they may be, are merely our opinions from where we sit, from our unique vantage point.

—

Does the right of the unborn supercede the right of the mother who is born already?

—

In competition, success is judged mostly by the score. In life, success has more to do with the quality of the participant. True success is often undetected by others. Humility is success. Honesty is success. Patience is success. My mother used to say, "You are already successful. Other people just don't know it yet."

—

Try to take everything in your life and use it as a chance to be better.

—

When there is controversy, agreement is not often possible. As human points of view, we cannot concur on everything. What is not only possible but necessary is for all of us to be able to understand viewpoints that are not our own even when we don't agree. It is imperative if we have any hope of moving forward as a society. In issues of race, we need to be able to understand the context of opposing views and need not be so laser focused on our issues that we forget that there are other races besides black and white that have their issues also. There are issues of gender, sexual orientation, religion, etc. Let's keep our minds open and remember that being "right" is not enough.

—

Talent brings precision and ease to an action. Character brings depth and purpose to that action. Character makes something positive of even what we would call a mistake.

—

In practice, we work on the musician that we want to be. Onstage, you show the musician that you are.

———

People who recognize their fears are more likely to prepare for the thing or things that make them afraid. People who deny their fears are more likely to make excuses.

———

An atheist is dependent upon the very same things as the Christian. Do not bicker because your names of those needs do not match.

———

Do not be discouraged because you cannot solve the ills and the problems of the big picture. Do all that you can to make the small picture, your immediate situation better.

———

Nurture you abilities and talents. Be vigilant for opportunity. The development of your skills is in your hands, but opportunity is not. Opportunity is always a gift.

———

Blessed is the man or woman who can show those considered the "least of us" that they are in the very same fraternity as "the best of us".

———

Always honor the downtrodden and the impoverished, because both of you have an opportunity to be each other's salvation.

—

Cherish the people in your life with the same passion and depth that you would if you were to lose them. Cherish your life the same way.

—

Art is not just for others. Art also teaches and nourishes the artist.

—

A cheater may sometimes seem to win but will never know true victory.

—

Teaching a young person to have pride in his or her school, team, neighborhood, family, appearance, job, etc. is very important, because teaching that youngster to have pride and respect for any or all of these is an indirect way of teaching pride and respect in oneself.

—

Discipline is a lesson impossible to teach effectively without teaching by example.

—

Even what NOT to do is a lesson taught by example.

—

I just found out yesterday that my Uncle John Gragg was the first black Captain of a ship in U.S. Army history, and it all made sense to me.

Uncle John's house, car, yard and everything were always spotless and immaculate! His ship was always the one used for dignitaries, because it was always the cleanest. A Captain has to lead by example. If he wants discipline from his crew, he must be the most disciplined.

Uncle John is the youngest looking 88 year old I have ever seen, a product of his good diet and exercise. He tends his own very large garden for hours every day! He doesn't let himself become idle. I left my Uncle's house with a firmer commitment to my own discipline.

Uncle John is still leading by example.

October 24, 2015

———

I find that every person's life is a story worth telling. And when that person tells that story, it is empowering, especially when he or she sees that their story, their life has impact. Tell your story!

———

Detail and focus are valuable tools, but they are double-edged swords. They both enable you to examine the particulars of life in depth, but too often they are at the expense of the bigger more important picture.

The pickpocket is aware of this when he or she taps you on the shoulder while taking your wallet from your purse or pocket. Detail can be both examination and distraction. Focus can be both concentration and misdirection. Do your best to never let your concentration be at the expense of the bigger more important picture.

———

Wise is the person who knows that Truth has many levels and chooses those levels wisely and with care. A woman who miscarries, for instance, does not need to hear the truth "that we all gotta go sometime."

———

Musicians! Entertainers! Being a "star" is pretend. If your audience believes it, you may have to take on that role. But do it with care, and never lose sight of the real truth…that you are no more and no less, no better or no worse than they are.

———

Us trying to explain eternity is similar to a grain of sand trying to explain the beach.

———

Quality can exist without quantity much better than quantity exists when there is little or no quality.

———

In music and in life, much of it depends upon the quality of the rests.

———

A note is the component of music, not music itself. Music is more than that. Music is beautiful order, strategic placement of notes and tones, melodies, themes, subtleties and harmonies. In fact, music is proof that those notes and tones have interacted with and been preceded by intelligence.

———

Being on time is the first step to being dependable. Dependability is the cornerstone of success. Honesty is your responsibility to truth and the foundation of character. Punctuality and dependability, honesty and character are all requirements if you want to be successful...and none of them require talent. You can have all of these with little talent and still find success. But even if you are blessed with a lot of talent, without these, your talent eventually is not enough, and your success is hard to maintain and on shaky ground.

———

I read somewhere that "Religion needs spirituality. Spirituality does not need religion."

———

We want our elected officials to do certain things, but as citizens we have responsibilities too. We also need to "reach across the aisle" and find common ground, to communicate without tearing down. Why should we expect from our leaders qualities that we ourselves do not exhibit?

———

Before you succumb to the urge to either gloat or mope, try to remember that neither of them helps.

———

Musicians and artists!

Music does what no other medium can do. Through the worst times in our history, music has been the thing that carried us through the struggle. From the Negro spirituals of slavery, to the Civil Rights movement's "We Shall Overcome", to Curtis Mayfield's "People Get Ready", from Mahalia Jackson's "Precious Lord", to John Lennon's "Give Peace A Chance", music has always helped us to endure and eventually overcome struggle, tragedy, and heartbreak. It is no different today. Music strengthens the oppressed and transforms society for the better.

So Musicians and Artists, be aware of the music that add to these troubling times. We possess the strongest tool the world has ever known for peace.

Let the soldiers take care of the violence. Let the politicians set their policies, while we as artists give people strength to go on, while we motivate and give hope to those who feel hopeless, while we nurture and grow the Peace. It is a high calling to be a musician or an artist...especially in these times.

———

It is good to have ideals. Having an ideal to live by is the most important part of honor, morality, and integrity. But having an ideal is not enough. It is only as good as its implementation. At best, having an ideal put to use is a show of character. At worst, an ideal is proclaimed and not lived up to...or even reversed because of fear...and that is hypocrisy. It takes courage to live up to your principles, even in times of danger.

———

Politicians are who they are largely because we, the people are who we are.

———

It easy to have principles when those principles are not tested.

———

A person with accurate facts who is unable to hear or even entertain the opinions or ideas of anyone besides his own is more detrimental to progress than one whose facts are lacking but is willing to listen to reason...in my opinion.

—

The world will be a much better place when the people who believe in peace are as active for their cause as the evil doers are for theirs.

—

Fashion is the passion that rations no emotion or supports the notion that beauty is merely skin deep. A designer is chin deep in color that's fuller, in style that's wild to those that don't know or don't go to the show where the models strut, where the designers put on a display that takes a locality and ignores the formalities to express the realities from the mind of design.

Fashion was once superficial to me, but now it's official to me that fashion is expression, like music and art. It comes from the heart of those who are brave and don't play it safe from the opinion of minions who still live in caves of stereotypes, inferior types, who would rather judge than be creative, rather sleep and be sedative, rather frown and drown in the safeness of convention, creating tension and dissension, because someone dared to step away from the crowd and say it out loud, "Here I am! This is ME!"

—

Aspirations and pipe dreams have the same goal. Only one of them has a plan. Dream big…and then get to work.

—

Worry can be useful if it initiates action or preparation.

—

You should have enthusiasm, but it should not be your strategy. You should also prepare for the possibility of your doubt's reality.

—

Ordinary goodness can do great things. It is important to know that virtue and character are already great, even when they are not connected to a deed.

—

We look to the soldiers to eradicate the evil doers, but it is up to us, the citizens, "we the people", to eradicate their ideology.

—

Your art is only as good as your audience's ability to understand it.

—

Today celebrates the birthday of Dr. Martin Luther King, Jr., but what does that celebration mean? I know what the holiday is for, and I agree that it should be celebrated, but how does it apply to each of us? How is it making a difference in our personal lives?

To me, Dr. Martin Luther King, Jr. is as important to American history as any President and more important than many of them. Martin's life helped this country to come closer to living up to its ideals of equality and justice. HE did his part, but what are we doing?

Everyone is not Martin, but there is much that we can do. We can mentor young people. We can give company and assistance to the elderly, help the homeless, and even if we don't offer the less fortunate money or shelter, we can at least treat them as if they are not invisible. Visit the Veterans. Volunteer. We can actually have a conversation with someone who has a different viewpoint than we do on controversial matters, rather than just seeking the company of those that agree with us already. If soldiers risk their lives for us, we should have the courage to risk our comfort and engage the controversial for the sake of forward progress.

There is much good that we can do, that we SHOULD do. Dr. Martin Luther King, Jr. lead by example, and we can too.

MLK Day, January 18, 2016

———

It is important to know who you are and of equal importance to know how who you are fits with other people.

———

The darkest cloud may do damage. It may bring rain, wind, flood, tornado, hurricane, thunder and lightning, snow and blizzard. Eventually, it will merely show us the beauty of the sunbeam.

———

I do not have a problem with Black History Month any more than I have a problem with Saint Patrick's Day. It is this Country's reminder that Black History is American History.

———

Whether or not you sit in first class, be first class.

———

Musicians should work on their character, especially the songwriters. Songwriters write about life, so we should know all we can about it and impact it as positively as possible. The artist who lives a life with purpose, insight, integrity, and care for their fellow man or woman is more likely to write meaningful music.

———

It is important to work on your craft and more important to work on the craftsman.

—

My father, by his example, showed me the value of humor and discipline. He did not know it, but it was two of his greatest gifts to me.

—

There are some things in life from which no one gets exemption.

—

Who are you? It is impossible to fully know the answer to that question but crucial that your answer be a favorable one.

—

Struggle focuses us. Defeat teaches us. Victory rewards us.

—

Music is the true essence of life, and because of that it retains the capacity to nurture and comfort us even when the circumstances of life are unfavorable and challenging.

—

It's tough, but try not to let your taste buds be your doctor.

—

Atheism does not have to be cynicism.

—

Be vigilant, as best you can, to never let technology get you to a place where you cannot do without it.

—

I am still here. There must be more to do

—

There is nothing more gratifying than seeing evidence that you raised your child well.

—

Knowledge is not the same as wisdom, and of the two, wisdom is greater. Life requires both, however.

—

Knowledge should always accompany wisdom. Knowledge void of wisdom is the foundation of the cynic.

—

Communication or the lack thereof consists of both what you say and how you say it.

—

Talent requires time to develop. Integrity does not.

—

The character of the artist multiplies and compounds the impact of the art.

—

Wisdom is more than just the facts. Wisdom is knowing what to do with the facts. One can have all the facts and still not have the truth.

—

What is time, except proof in the linear world that Zero is alive and well.

—

Which came first, the Life or the Love? Don't worry about it. Enjoy them both.

—

Christianity does not have to be "holier than thou".

—

My belief is that Life and Love exist together, that they are the intent of the other. If Life sustains us, why wouldn't it follow that it loves us too?

—

Time is a device for measuring Eternity, but it is not the same thing. Like all tools, it will be put down when its task is complete.

—

People are not created to agree on everything. We are here to respect each other's differences.

—

Our society is not damaged because we have varying opinions. Society is harmed when we have intolerance for those who do not think like us or agree with us.

———

As a society, the only thing more dangerous than the loss of some of our privacy is a terrorist with his or her privacy, because a terrorist with the ability to act in secrecy can end our chances of even having the debate.

———

In democracy, the majority wins, but that does not insure that the majority is right. Sometimes the rational thinkers are in the minority.

———

All meaningful cultural exchange comes with some level of discomfort and dissent.

———

Do your best to be on the morally right side of every issue you are aware of, for morality is the basis of character.

———

If cow's milk were so good for your bones it would not have to be fortified with vitamin D.

———

How you treat and how you communicate with those whose opinions diametrically oppose yours tell a lot about your character.

———

Man was created with Love, and Love will endure after man is gone. Love is the Alpha and Omega.

—

Any system of government is only as good as the people running it. Greed and lust for power will ruin any government and any system of government.

—

Do your best to never let the truth be brutal. Diplomacy and tact, if at all possible...

—

Life must teach us
    So truth can reach us
In our hearts there
    Must be new birth

For love is the answer
    And hate is the chance
And we are the
    Saviors of the Earth

Life must teach us
    So truth can reach us
As the flag of our
    Freedom unfurls

For love is the answer
    And hate is the cancer
And we are the
    Saviors of the world

—

Americans fought and died for the right to vote. I don't think they fought for the right of the Electoral College to vote for them.

—

People need a true leader, not just a ruler.

—

An empty smile can be much sadder than no smile at all.

—

Sometimes dissent, controversy, and turmoil is the precursor to societal growth and advancement, the awkward unbalanced period, the cultural puberty before the maturation of a generation. Other times it is an attempt to prevent the same. Time will tell...

—

The optimistic mature person looks for the silver lining and the lesson in adversity. The pessimist immature person wonders why he or she was chosen for the hardship and looks to create an educated complaint.

—

Like music, no matter how great the solo, no matter how masterful the improvisation, it must eventually come to an end. No thing, nothing lasts forever. Think about that...

—

Beauty has to be felt if it is to be seen.

—

More important than who you will vote for is who you will be before and after the election. The vote will come and go, but who you are will last your lifetime.

—

What is the quality of your silence?

—

Rhythm is a meaningful zero. By itself, it is nothing, but it is the nothing that the rest of music is built upon.

—

Life is infinite. It cannot be fully explained, but it can be experienced. The vastness of Life exists beyond our abilities to fully define it and therefore must be lived always with an element of faith.

—

You can never legislate a society into morality nor tax them into prosperity, yet they are both necessary.

—

Do not be so laser focused on reaching your goals that you compromise your principles to achieve them.

—

Be more concerned for your content than your appearance, but let one reflect the other.

—

Music is the greatest tool for Peace that the world has ever known, and that makes the artist and the musician the greatest agent of Peace that this world has right now.

—

Let's care for each other more and criticize each other less.

—

You can't complain about not achieving your success when you won't fulfill the things that don't even require talent...like being on time, being dependable, being easy to work with, being prepared, etc. If you won't do these things do you really deserve success?

—

Your words mean very little until your actions lead the way.

—

We are backward in that we undervalue the things we have a lot of like sunsets, health, family, friends, freedom, etc., and put too much emphasis on the trivial, the petty, and the unimportant.

—

You have to be successful on the inside to be truly successful on the outside.

—

Playing music takes talent. Having a career in music requires so much more.

—

No one gets a chance to live their whole life without dealing with real life eventually.

—

Before you look down on a drug addict, ask yourself how you handle your own sugar consumption. Addiction is addiction. (Nicotine too!)

—

It is important to be grateful and thankful, for it is certain that we will handle with care the things of which we are appreciative.

—

You rebuild trust with time, not just words, no matter how sincere.

—

You have a right to choose the life you want, but the effects of that life on others is not entirely up to you.

—

We see the goodness of others with our own goodness.

—

Whatever you do, do it with honor.

—

Life benefits from the goodness that exists, not just the goodness that is seen. If you have the chance to do a good deed, even if no one is there to see it, do it anyway.

—

When people are afraid they are too often willing to sacrifice their values and principles for the feeling of safety.

—

There are few things more revealing than repeated denials of something that you were never accused of.

—

Be careful of your condemnation of drug addicts. Too many of us are in a similar manner addicted to sugar and simple carbohydrates. Both addictions have catastrophic consequences.

—

If you can't make someone feel important, do your best to at least make them feel significant.

—

What good is it to be talented if your abilities fail to help others?

—

From humble beginnings come great things.

—

The Past, the Future…most importantly, the Present.

—

It is immeasurable what it means to know that you are loved and respected.

—

Financially, I am not wealthy, but I AM rich!!!

—

Do not miss the essence of music by concentrating only on the notes. Do not miss the essence of life by concentrating only on the events.

—

Today let us be thankful for the things we have and less memorable about the things we wish we had. For today, let's celebrate our similarities more than we debate our differences. Let us have care for those less fortunate. Also, let us remember and acknowledge those who are not here anymore that helped us to become the people we are.

—

If you are lucky enough to live to be 100 years old, you will have lived 36, 525 days (counting the leap year days). If you had a dollar for every day you were to be alive and you knew that you would get no more, would you be more careful in spending your dollars than you are in spending your days?

—

Sometimes wealth has nothing to do with money.

—

Gratitude unlocks the fulness of life. It can turn what we have into enough and more.

—

The average person runs from danger. A policeman runs towards danger. A fireman runs toward danger. A soldier runs into danger. When someone puts your safety ahead theirs, the least you can do is show your gratitude when you are in their presence.

—

You can tell a lot about a person by how he or she accepts punishment for the wrongdoing he or she is responsible for.

—

If God Himself deems you worthy, who are you to say otherwise?

—

I just played in the 2016 Rock & Roll Hall of Fame induction ceremony at the Barclay's Center in Brooklyn, New York, and as exciting as it was, it was not more gratifying than speaking to the young 5th-8th graders two days before in Newark, New Jersey.

—

True wealth has nothing to do with money.

—

It is important that we have good journalism and a functioning free press, for having an informed society is absolutely essential if the majority rule of Democracy is to prevent itself from descending into mob rule.

A painter seldom uses a broad brush to create details on the canvas. In life, your heart paints with a broad brush and similarly is seldom the best tool when making decisions requiring detail and nuance.

—

Diplomacy and tact are two condiments of communication that make the truth more palatable.

—

To get to the "birth" of the rest of your life, sometimes you must go through the "labor" of divorce.

—

My life falls into three categories.
    1. Who I am
    2. Who I am as a musician/artist
    3. My career
Of the three, the first is most important.

—

Opposition is a learning tool to help educate us with experience about Oneness.

—

It is not enough to have a strong opinion if you are not knowledgeable about differing or counter opinions. Even being "right" is detrimental if it makes you more closed minded.

Everything that comes to an end is just a tool to teach us about what doesn't come to an end.

—

Music will go on, but it will not be the same. That is the nature of music. It outlives the musician.

Prince is gone. His music lasts forever. There are no more James Browns. No more Sinatras. No more Elvis. No more Hendrix. No more MJ's...and now sadly, no more Prince...but the music endures...the musician dies, but the music always goes on...

Rest in Peace, Prince
Rest in Purple Peace
April 21, 2016

—

Now that the Christmas holiday is over, let's continue to spread the good will. In place of "Merry Christmas" let's now say "Have a nice day", "Thank you so much" or "I look forward to seeing you next time." Good will is at its best when it is not only expressed here and there. Christmas shows us how we should be all the time. We are good people, but let's be better.

—

Thank you to each and every Veteran. You have fought the fight for us so that we can live our lives in peace. For that I say thank you!

—

Music is a musician's interaction with immortality.

—

Let's love each other…and in the meantime…let's try to keep the meantime from being the "mean" time.

—

The Zero is more than nothing or no things. Time is the non thing that gives things order and a chance to experience. Space is nothingness that gives things the room to operate. Nothing can exist without the gifts of the void, because Zero is both order and opportunity.

—

It is not important always to smile, but, if at all possible, do your best to remain positive and optimistic, smile or not.

—

Days after Prince's death, I heard that there was a push to put Prince on the new twenty dollar bill and change its value to 19.99 and call it "the bill formerly known as the twenty".
I said that we should put James Brown on the dollar bill, since he has ALWAYS been "On the One"!!!

—

Self confidence must always contain some element of humility or it too easily descends into mere bravado or pompous bluster.

—

What greater deed is there than for an adult to teach a young person to be a better person by setting a good example?

—

I am such an optimist that even my blood type is B Positive.

—

Even the right choices have consequences.

—

An electron cannot force itself to be hydrogen. It is given the opportunity to be hydrogen by the zero at the center of the nucleus. Zero gives the existence of the electron purpose.

—

Who can be wholly and rightfully against racism or any prejudice if that person is tolerant of sexism, gender bias, forgetful of the Native American, insensitive to sexual orientation, or looks down on the poor? The problem does not rest only in the inequity that bothers you the most. It rests in ALL forms of man's inhumanity to man. Do your best NOT to let your hatred of whatever the unfairness give you tunnel vision, blinding you to the rest of the world's injustices and inequities.

—

Life is a constant "What's next?"

—

Everyday is epic if you take the time to notice.

—

Who deserves to be rich that won't do what they can to help, protect, or defend the poor?

—

"One of these days" is the most elusive time frame.

———

Improvement by yourself can often be done with merely a change of heart. To improve as a couple or as a group involves not only a change of heart but a change of procedure.

———

The bully who tried to pick a fight by declaring, "There's nothing between us except space and opportunity…" had no idea how profound that statement was.

———

Individuality can indeed expand the infinite, but it cannot confine it.

———

Your battle against injustice is incomplete, no matter how sincere, if you fight against one form of inequity or unfairness while allowing another to perpetuate.

———

Love at first sight is possible, indeed. But a meaningful relationship requires more than the initial viewing.

———

The properties of Zero are cohesiveness, stability, and order.
The arena of Zero is space.
The gift of Zero and space is opportunity.
The magic of zero, space, and opportunity is creativity.
The creative Zero gives us the essence of beauty…

Because it loves us so…

—

Never become so concerned with nutrition that you lose your ability to eat peacefully with immense gratitude for whatever is on your plate.

Food like Life, is never a given. It is always privilege.

—

Not all are poor because of flawed decision making or laziness.

—

I am of the mindset that the key to solving or moving past our differences is respecting each other while we talk about them and attempt to work them out.

—

Change is not always easy, but it is necessary.

—

I continue to feel that people who talk to each other, even if their opinions differ, can learn from each other.

—

We are more likely to love those we are familiar with, more likely to be familiar with those that we talk to, and more likely to talk to those we interact with. We can solve any problem if we just take the time to get to know one another.

—

Any meaningful solution starts first with a look in the mirror.

———

Everyone has a doctorate in their own opinions. Too many get an F on their knowledge of the opinions of others.

———

Being respectful should not be based upon the actions of others. Disrespect lacks maturity. Like a child, we say, "He started it!", as if it gives us permission to lack the character and discipline we need to constructively move forward.

———

I do my best to live a life of discipline and respect for everyone. I admit that I am far from perfect, but I believe in the potential goodness of people, even when they seem to be doing their best to make me feel otherwise.

———

Sometimes it takes your respect and discipline to bring out the same in others. Why should we let the immature and undisciplined actions of others give us permission to lose our self control?

———

Ending conflict is more important than who started it.

———

Racism, sexism, violence, injustice, etc., are difficult, highly emotional issues. The maintaining of our respect and self control is absolutely necessary for us to move out of just reacting to these issues and into actually solving them.

Communication is as much listening as it is making a good point. "Being right" is not enough when people's opinions differ, especially when the stakes and emotions are high.

—

If we respect each other, we have a chance of moving forward. Disrespect is a problem on its own. It widens the divide and deepens the animosity.

—

Do your best never to be so concerned with nutrition that you lose your ability to enjoy your meal.

—

I disagree that our country is more divided than it has ever been. Our differences are just on the surface now. It was MUCH more divided when there were separate water fountains, and separate toilets, separate restaurants and theaters, women could not vote, Blacks could not vote, gays could not marry nor serve in the military, etc.

It is now okay to be gay and lesbian and in love, and transgenders don't have to stay hidden. What we are seeing and feeling are growing pains. We are in a state of cultural puberty, temporarily somewhere between adolescence and maturity as a country. Our differences are out in the open now, and this discomfort, this awkward necessity, gives us a chance to be better than we have ever been.

—

171

The attitude that police are never wrong is as much a part of the problem as the fact that people break the law.

—

Offering statistics to a suffering individual instead of caring and empathy is clear evidence of a lack of compassion.

—

Our words matter. Our actions matter. Use both carefully, because the times are too incendiary.

—

Evil shouts louder than peace, but do not be fooled by its wailing to believe that evil is stronger. Evil will have its moments, but know that evil, no matter how destructive, like a storm, eventually will merely show the beauty of the sunbeam.

—

If the government is responsible for caring for our infrastructure, our roads, buildings, and bridges…how can government NOT be responsible for caring for its people…especially the poor and those in need. People are more important than roads, buildings, and bridges.

—

A ball thrown against the wall rebounds at almost the same speed that it was thrown. The same with racism. The rebound of the ball may do damage, but it is not as big of a problem as the fact that the ball was thrown in the first place.

—

The United States Constitution says, "of the people", "by the people", and most importantly, "for the people". That includes people in need, of all ages, colors, sexual orientations, and genders.

——

It does not take the proper leaders for the people to be who they should be.

——

Love without familiarity is too often shallow and fallible.

——

The collective "we" are the first problem. The leaders follow and go where the people allow them.

——

The value of protest is seldom seen at the time of the protest.

——

The gifts of a good parent endure long after the parent is gone.

——

While there is no tragedy, let us learn tragedy's lesson…that we need each other. And because we need each other…let us respect each other…not because we agree on everything, but because life is fragile, life is a gift, and things can change at any moment.

——

You can dislike the President, but you should not disrespect the Presidency…two different things.

—

We are all in this together.

—

We are bound by humanity and separated by politics. Humanity is more important than politics.

—

Nobody can have every perspective.

—

Beware! Opinions do a very good job of masquerading as knowledge, and perspective, especially our perspective, too often, wears the facade of the big picture or the whole story.

—

Write music about the truth because the truth is timeless and irresistible.

—

If you want information
    Look at the facts
If you want the truth
    Look between the facts and
Understand their context

—

To oppress the masses,
    Ignorance is essential.

One who has knowledge of self and a feel for how he or she relates
    to others,
Can never be fully oppressed.

———

I have a hard time believing that wide spread ignorance is a
random mistake.

———

The top tenth of
    One percent
They own it all
    And the Establishment
They don't care at all
    They benefit
Because they write the law
    And if you don't own a cent
You're invisible

———

There are no downsides to music. However, there are many
downsides to a career in music.

———

Having someone who believe in you deepens your belief in
yourself.

———

Facts are finite and truth is not, kind of like notes in music. The
note is real, but it is far from telling the story of the whole song.
Notes can help you to experience music, but the music, the feeling,

that experience, is something else entirely and goes beyond the notes. The same thing goes for facts.

—

Time, to me, seems to be a tool of Creation that insures that everything in life has context. Take away time and you lose perspective. Without time there is no "here" and "there" for the only difference between "here" or "there" is the time it takes to get from one to the other.

—

The world is not entirely corrupted, but corruption and evil get much bigger news. Look on the highway. Most everyone drives as they should...but we count the accidents and fatalities. This world is more full of respectful loving people than violent corrupt ones.

—

Perspective can change the facts. Clockwise is counter-clockwise to the face of the clock. So, speak on the facts with an open mind. From another perspective it could not only be different but just the opposite.

—

Facts are finite. Truth is infinite.
   Facts are clues, but they do not tell
   the whole story.
Facts are true, but they are not the whole truth.

—

Music is beyond the notes. In a like manner, Truth is beyond the facts.

—

Let us remember who we are on Christmas and extend it into the rest of the year.

—

It is easier to vilify someone that we disagree with than to sit down with that person and attempt to work out your differences.

—

Immense love or immense hate are both their own brand of tribute. Strong love and strong hate both require you to focus on the person above all others.

—

It is important not to miss the point when you argue the "facts".

—

When expressing the "facts" or your opinion of the facts, do your best to recount them with the wisdom of diplomacy.

—

Discussion is healthy. We are better off when we express our differences out loud and maintain respect for each other.

—

I am fortunate enough to get a chance to experience much beauty in my life, so I do my best to share it.

—

The Left and the Right are divided politically,
    but they are united in that
    neither adequately address the issues
    of the poorest of us.
This Country is divided from Left to Right
    but also from top to bottom

—

Poverty has repercussions that ALL of us feel.
    Poverty breeds crime.
    Poverty breeds violence.
    Poverty magnifies bigotry.
The extreme reality of poverty breeds
    extremism.
Yes, let's heal our political differences, but let
    us also remember the ones most vulnerable.

—

We should listen to each other, because no one can have
everybody's perspective, and everyone's perspective has value.

—

A fact should lead one towards the truth, not obscure it.

—

Having ideals and living up to them often requires a measure of
risk. It was always risky potentially to say, "Bring us your tired and
your poor…"

—

Being negative is like stomping on your own toes and complaining
about the pain.

—

Don't go into the music business if the only thing you plan on improving is your music.

—

Righteousness is powerful, because if you are in its presence, it is irresistible. One can move the masses with righteousness.

—

It is easier for the minority to rule when the majority is in conflict.

—

More important than knowing where you come from, is knowing who you are now. Both are related, and both are important. One is in the past, and one is in the present. Yes, learn about your past, but live in the present.

—

There is something wrong with a country where the top tenth of one percent owns the same amount of wealth as the bottom ninety percent combined…and the bottom one tenth of one percent has no wealth at all.

—

By the way…
God DID create Adam and Steve…

And He loves them both…

—

Your reputation is not up to you. It is based on the opinions of others, and people do have a right to think what they like.

But, your reality, who you really are, is not only in your power but is your responsibility.

—

Vehemently disagreeing with someone does not require nor give you license to be vehemently disagreeable.

—

God DID create Adam and Steve
God DID create Adam and Eve
God DID create Adam and Adam
God DID create Eve and Eve
God DID create Adam who is now Eve
God DID create Eve who is now Adam

And He loves them all…

—

An exception to the rule does not negate nor weaken the rule. To me, lesbians, gays, bisexuals, and transgenders are all just exceptions to the assumed rule of heterosexuality. They pose no threat and are their own special kind of beauty.

We should be defined NOT by our sexuality but by our humanity.

—

If loving Stephanie was against the law or against your religion…
If you felt that my love for her was "sin" according to your scripture…
I would still respect you…
But…
I would be one law breaking religion abominating man!

We should love and respect each other more
And...
Judge each other less.

—

Love is love...
No matter who you love.

—

Imagine your love for your wife or husband was against the Bible
or any Holy Book. You could not, and would not, nor should not
change it.
Love is love, no matter who you love.

—

All of us should be on the list of inclusion. The problem is that
too many of us have our own special lists of who should be excluded.

—

Two cents well spent are worth more than two hundred dollars
misspent or spent dishonestly.

—

God does not need our help with judgement, but HE does need
our help when it comes to how we treat each other.

—

Who should have to open a Bible or any religious book before they exhibit simple kindness or respect for their fellow citizens?

—

It is amazing to me how divisive a call for respect and acceptance can be.
I believe the majority wants us to come together.
I believe the ones who want divisiveness are in the minority.
So...
By our actions...
Let the majority rule.

—

Sometimes, you get a wolf in sheep's clothing.
Other times, the wolf is just a wolf.

—

Sometimes, being "right" is the wrong thing to do.

—

I MATTER

This song is for...
The one that's not the champion
    The one that has been trampled on
And maybe you don't have a home
    And your name is unknown
You don't get enough publicity
    Or you're not the right ethnicity
Or maybe you don't know your mother
    Or not as famous as your brother

This is what you've got to do
    See that no one means more than you
And even when you're fed up
    You've got to keep your head up and say
I am here
I am here
    And I Matter...

This song is for...
    The struggling single mother
And the chemically addicted
    The physically constricted
And the wrongfully convicted
    I can't say I know your pain
I won't say that I do
    But behind even the darkest cloud
There's a sky that is blue
    And the sun shines too
The toughest pressure makes a diamond
    And that diamond is you
So even when you're down and out
    From the highest mountain you shout
I am here
I am here
    And I matter...

I never could dance like Michael
I can't sing like Stevie
   And sometimes when I speak my truth
I swear that people don't believe me
   I never could dunk a basketball
I can't rap like Ludacris at all
   Sometimes it's just me and my songs
Staring at an empty wall

   But this is what I've got to see
See that no one means more than me
   And one day when my days are numbered
Headed to my final slumber

I'll say that I was here…
I was here…
And I mattered…
(And you matter too…)

About the Author

Joseph Allen Wooten (keyboardist, vocalist, songwriter, arranger, composer, producer, educator, and motivational speaker) is a 3-time Grammy nominated artist who has been the keyboardist for The Steve Miller Band since 1993. He is also the brother of bass player Victor Wooten (5 time Grammy Award Winner), Roy Wooten aka "Futureman"(5 time Grammy Award Winner), Regi Wooten aka "The Teacha", and Rudy "Quiet Storm" Wooten (1958-2010).

Born to Dorothy and Elijah "Pete" Wooten, Joseph is the 2nd youngest of 5 Wooten Brothers, all of whom are musicians.

Joseph's early elementary school years were spent with his siblings playing nightclubs and sharing the stage with Curtis Mayfield, War and other major artists of the time as "The Wooten Brothers". In the '70s there were more major artists to share the stage with; The Temptations, The SOS Band, Stephanie Mills, Dexter Wansel, Ramsey Lewis, Maze featuring Frankie Beverly, and others.

During the 80s, Joseph and his brothers had a residency at Busch Gardens in Williamsburg, Virginia, where Joseph honed his skills not only as a keyboardist, but as an accordion player. He wrote, composed, arranged, and performed with the orchestra over 40 pieces of music for every individual cast member.
The brothers caught the ear of the popular R&B artist/producer Kashif where they recorded an album entitled "The Wootens" for Arista Records. Joseph's unmatched talent and undeniable groove landed him the position of band leader and keyboardist for Kashif. During that time, he also sang background vocals for Whitney Houston on her Grammy nominated debut album, "Whitney", as well as Kenny G.'s "Gravity" album. Joseph was a co-writer of Kashif's Grammy nominated R&B instrumental "Call Me Tonight" and also contributed numerous compositions to brother Victor's Grammy nominated CD, "Yin Yang".

In '93 he became the keyboard player/vocalist for the legendary Steve Miller Band, playing large venues around the world. When not on the road with Rock & Roll Hall of Fame inductee Steve Miller, Joseph is a part of another elite group of handpicked musicians called Freedom Sings, a multi-media experience celebrating The First Amendment and free expression, organized by Ken Paulson (former editor-in-chief of USA Today).

In between breaks from his extensive travels with the Steve Miller Band, he also makes music with the Wooten Brothers, performs with with his brother, Victor, and leads his own band, Joseph Wooten & The Hands Of Soul.

When not traveling from city to city, Joseph can often be found speaking to college, high school, middle school, and elementary school students about character development, self-esteem, self-respect, and personal growth using his own life experiences as examples.□

22214167R00119

Made in the USA
Columbia, SC
29 July 2018